At David C Cook, we equip the local church around
the corner and around the globe to make disciples.
Come see how we are working together—go to
www.davidccook.com. Thank you!

transforming lives together

The PROMISES of GOD

R. C. SPROUL

The PROMISES of GOD

DISCOVERING THE ONE WHO
KEEPS HIS WORD

transforming lives together

THE PROMISES OF GOD
Published by David C Cook
4050 Lee Vance Drive
Colorado Springs, CO 80918 U.S.A.

David C Cook U.K., Kingsway Communications
Eastbourne, East Sussex BN23 6NT, England

The graphic circle C logo is a registered trademark of David C Cook.

The website addresses recommended throughout this book are offered as a
resource to you. These websites are not intended in any way to be or imply an
endorsement on the part of David C Cook, nor do we vouch for their content.

Unless otherwise noted, all Scripture quotations in the main text
are taken from the New King James Version®. Copyright © 1982 by
Thomas Nelson, Inc. Used by permission. All rights reserved.

Unless otherwise noted, all Scripture quotations in the chapter study
guides are taken from The Holy Bible, English Standard Version®
(ESV®), copyright © 2001 by Crossway, a publishing ministry of
Good News Publishers. Used by permission. All rights reserved.

LCCN 2013938887
Paperback ISBN 978-0-8307-7206-3
Hardcover ISBN 978-1-4347-0423-8
eISBN 978-1-4347-0602-7

© 2013, 2018 R. C. Sproul
Published in association with the literary agency of Wolgemuth & Associates, Inc.

The Team: Alex Field, Nick Lee, Renada Arens, Karen Athen
Cover Design: Amy Konyndyk
Cover Photo: istockphoto.com

Printed in the United States of America
Paperback Edition 2018

1 2 3 4 5 6 7 8 9 10

102617

CONTENTS

PREFACE

Sometimes historic Reformed theology is called covenant theology. It is true that there is a certain focus on the covenants within Reformed theology. However, I have never really appreciated this nickname very much because I believe that all branches of theology, to some degree, recognize the importance of the biblical covenants in understanding redemption. In other words, the covenants form the basic structure of redemptive history.

The key function of the covenants in redemption history is the relationship between promise and fulfillment. We exist as the people of God because He has made and kept promises to His people. We can be a part of the family of God only because our God makes and keeps covenants. God never breaks or changes His promises. They are everlasting promises to which God committed Himself forever. For example, when Mary, under the influence of the Holy Spirit, sang her *Magnificat*, she declared that God had remembered the promise that He had made to Abraham (Luke

1:54–55). Mary understood her place in church history in terms of the fulfillment of a covenant.

The hardest thing in the world for the Christian is to live by faith rather than by sight. It is difficult because we never see God. We are not eyewitnesses of the resurrection, as the first-century Apostles were. We live on the basis of the testimony of those who went before us, which means that we must walk by faith. We are justified by faith, and that means by trusting the Word of God. However, it is one thing to believe in God—to believe that there is a God—and quite another thing to believe God. But living faith involves trusting the promises of God.

Even when everything around us seems to testify to the futility of our lives, causing us to lose hope, we are in a covenant relationship with God. Therefore, we are people who live by trust in His promises. We break our promises to one another. We break our promises to God. But God never breaks His promises to us. Throughout history, God has demonstrated that He is supremely trustworthy. That's why, in one sense, nothing could be more foolish than not to trust in the promises of God.

I hope that this book on God's biblical covenants will help you trust in all of God's promises. We worship and serve a covenant-making and covenant-keeping God, and He is worthy of all our trust.

—R. C. Sproul
Sanford, Florida
September 2012

1

THE MEANING
OF COVENANT

The concept of covenant is integral and foundational to the divine revelation. We could even say that God reveals His Word and His plan biblically through the structure of various covenants. The covenants are prominent in the Old Testament and play a significant role in the teaching of the New Testament.

Despite the prominence of this structure, there is much confusion over the meaning of the term *covenant*. For example, we speak frequently about the difference between the old covenant and the new covenant, but we also speak of the Old Testament and the New Testament, and we have a tendency to use those terms interchangeably, seeing "Old Testament" as a synonym for "old covenant" and "New Testament" as a synonym for "new covenant."

Of course, these terms are closely related, but they are not really synonyms. They do not mean exactly the same thing.

There is also confusion because of the ways in which the idea of covenant is handled in twenty-first-century cultures. For instance, covenants were quite foundational for the United States as a nation. The political theory that was implemented in the grand experiment that is the United States relied heavily on John Locke's idea of the social contract. This concept held that there is a relationship between the rulers and those who are ruled, between the government and the people, whereby the leaders are selected or elected by the people and are empowered to rule only by the consent of the people. In essence, there is an agreement, a mutual promise of fidelity, between the people, who pledge their allegiance to their government, and the government officials, who take oaths of office to uphold the Constitution. There is a contract or a pact, an agreement binding these two sides to each other.

In addition, we often talk about the industrial contract, which comes in many forms. When a person goes to work for a company, he may sign a contract wherein the employer promises him certain remuneration, benefits, and so on, and wherein the employee promises to give so much of his time in working for the company. We see this kind of covenant in labor agreements. Also, on a more popular level, every time we buy something with a credit card or on an installment basis, we enter into a contract or an agreement to pay the full amount for the merchandise or the service over time. Even more significant is the marriage contract, an agreement that involves oaths and vows, sanctions and promises, between two people. All of these agreements are covenants.

Now, all of these covenants have elements of similarity to the biblical covenants, but they are not identical. Though the biblical covenants have elements of promise, one thing makes them different from these other kinds of agreements—biblical covenants are established on the basis of a divine sanction. That is, they are established not on the foundation of promises made by equal parties, but on the foundation of the divine promise of God. In the biblical covenants, it is God who declares the terms and makes the promises.

THE STRUCTURE OF REVELATION

The covenants provide the structure of redemptive history, the context in which God works out His plan of redemption. This fundamental idea was upheld for many centuries, but it became the focus of controversy in the middle of the twentieth century. Rudolf Bultmann (1884–1976), a higher-critical scholar in Germany, made a distinction between what he called *heilsgeschichte*, or "salvation history," and history itself. When he spoke of *heilsgeschichte*, he meant something that took place not on the horizontal plane of world history but above history, in some sort of supratemporal realm. Bultmann embraced an existential form of philosophy and believed that salvation happens not on this level but vertically—as he put it, immediately and directly from above. He saw salvation as a mystical thing that happens when a person has a crisis experience of faith.

At the same time, he said that the Bible is filled with both mythology and real history, but in order for the Bible to have any meaning for us today, it must be demythologized. That is, we have to tear off the husk of myth that holds that kernel of historical truth. So, he consigned anything that smacked of the supernatural—such as the virgin birth, the miracles of Jesus, the resurrection, and so on—to the realm of myth, not the realm of history.

The whole point of that kind of existential thinking and theology that drove the German theologians in the twentieth century was that salvation does not have to be rooted and grounded in history in order to be real. We can still have the "Christ-event," which is an existential moment that people experience, a moment of crisis. But that idea is far removed from the biblical concept of redemption.

Oscar Cullman (1902–1999), the Swiss theologian and New Testament scholar, wrote a trilogy of books in the middle of the twentieth century concerning this matter of redemptive history. The first book was called *Christ and Time*. In it he examined the time-frame references of the Bible, such as years, days, hours, and so on. The second book was on the person of Christ. The third book was titled *Salvation in History*, which was a comprehensive rebuttal of Bultmann, arguing that the Scriptures see God's revelation as inexorably bound up with real history. The Dutch New Testament scholar Herman Ridderbos (1909–2007) seconded that motion and argued that the Bible is not written like an ordinary history book. It is not simply a chronology of the actions of the Hebrew people. It's more than that. It is indeed the unfolding of the drama of God's work of redemption—so it is appropriate to call the Bible redemptive history. Whereas the critics were saying, "The Bible's not history; it's *redemptive* history," Cullman, Ridderbos, and others were saying, "Yes, it's redemptive history, but it's redemptive *history*." The fact that the Bible is concerned with redemption is no excuse to rip it out of the context of real history.

The Bible is filled with allusions to real history. When we come to the New Testament documents, we come first to the accounts of the birth of Christ, the famous Christmas story. We read: "And it came to pass in those days that a decree went out from Caesar Augustus that all the world should be registered. This census first took place while Quirinius was governing Syria" (Luke 2:1–2). In other words, Luke placed the setting for the birth of Christ in real history. People such as Pontius Pilate, Caiaphas, and others were real historical personages. The pharaoh of Egypt, Cyrus, Belshazzar, and Nebuchadnezzar were all real historical figures. So, the Bible talks about God's working in and through the normal plane of history.

In the first book of his trilogy, *Christ and Time*, Cullmann made a distinction between two Greek words for "time." *Chronos* is the ordinary Greek word that refers to the moment-by-moment passing of time. I wear what we commonly call a wristwatch, but the more technical term for it is a chronometer. A chronometer is something that measures *chronos*, the passing of seconds, minutes, and hours.

The other word, *kairos*, has a special meaning. It has to do not simply with history but with what we would call the historic.

Everything that happens in time is historical, but not everything that happens is historic. We use the term *historic* to refer to specific moments in time that are pregnant in their significance and meaning, moments that change everything. The attack on Pearl Harbor on December 7, 1941, was a historic moment in American history. It changed our culture forever. September 11, 2001, also changed our national culture forever. It, too, was a historic moment. But both of these moments, these *kairotic* events, took place not in some "never-never land" of existential, gnostic thinking, but in the actual plane of history.

At the heart of the biblical announcement of the coming of the Messiah is the statement that Jesus came in "the fullness of time" (Gal. 4:4). The Greek word used there is *pleroma*; it has to do with a kind of fullness that indicates satiation. If I put a glass under a faucet and filled it to the rim with water, that glass's state of fullness would not equal *pleroma*. I would have to leave the glass under the faucet until one more drop would cause the water in the glass to spill out; that would be *pleroma*. It is fullness so full that there is no room for another ounce or another speck of anything to be added. That helps us understand what the Bible means when it says that in the plan of God, Christ came in the "fullness of time."

That idea is inseparably related to the gospel itself. When the Apostles addressed the gospel in their preaching in the book of Acts or in their letters, they talked about how God had prepared history for the coming of His Son. Everything in Old Testament history, before the birth of Christ, moved toward that *kairotic* moment. Everything after the death, resurrection, and ascension of Christ refers back to those *kairotic* moments that shaped the whole future of the people of God. But the context of redemption is real history, not some spiritual realm that is outside the measurable views of history as we know it.

THE HEBREW CONCEPT OF COVENANT

In the Old Testament, the word that is translated by the English word *covenant* is the word *berîyth*. The New Testament, however, is written in Greek. The Greek translation of the Old Testament, the Septuagint, was produced by exilic Jews during the Hellenization process of Alexander the Great, which had the subjugated nations and peoples speaking Greek. Lest the sacred Scriptures of the Hebrews be lost to the Jewish people who were being forced to speak Greek, a team of seventy Jewish scholars came together and translated the Hebrew scriptures into Greek. That was a very important event in the history of Judeo-Christianity, because there we begin to see how Old Testament concepts were rendered into the Greek language, a language that was not native to the people of the old covenant. The Septuagint, then, is almost like a key to a code, because by it we can see how the Jews translated their own scriptures into Greek, and then compare how the New Testament writers used the same language.

One of the problems that the Jews who produced the Septuagint struggled with was choosing a Greek word to render the Hebrew *berîyth* into the Greek language. There were no words that really matched the Hebrew term *berîyth*, which is now translated by the English word *covenant*. The choice came down to a couple of words, and the one that won the day was *diathēkē*. For the most part, *diathēkē* is used in the New Testament to translate the Hebrew word *berîyth* or the Hebrew concept of covenant.

This word, *diathēkē*, is the source of some of the confusion between "old covenant" and "Old Testament," and "new covenant" and "New Testament." The reason is that *diathēkē* can be translated not only as "covenant," but also as "testament." However, at the time of the Septuagint, a testament in the Greek culture had a couple of things that made it significantly different from the Old Testament concept of covenant. First, in the Greek culture, a testament was something that could be changed at any time by the testator, as long as the testator was alive. A person could make up his last will and testament, become angry with his designated heirs, and write them out of his will. I say this to my children: "You're out of the will!" Of course, I am just joking when I say that, but it actually does happen that people are disinherited, written out of people's wills. But when God makes a covenant with His people, He can punish them for breaking His covenant, but He never abandons the covenant promises that He makes.

The second reason why *diathēkē* was a poor choice is that the benefits of a testament do not accrue until after the testator dies. But when God enters into covenant with people, they do not have to wait for Him to die to inherit the blessings from that covenant, because He's incapable of dying. So, with those two great weaknesses, we wonder why the Septuagint translators chose the Greek word *diathēkē* to translate the Hebrew *berîyth*.

This is significant for us because the Hebrews conceived of a covenant not simply as an agreement, but as an agreement plus the divine promise, which rests ultimately on the integrity of God, not on us as weak covenant partners. This is very important for our understanding of the covenant promises of God.

The other Greek word that was considered to translate *berîyth* in the Septuagint was *sunkatathesis*. It has the prefix *sun-* or *syn-*, which we encounter in the English words *synonym, syncretism, synchronization,* and the like; it simply means "with." The idea of *sunkatathesis* in the Greek culture was an agreement between equal partners. But the Hebrews would have none of that. They did not want to use that as the translation of the *berîyth* because they wanted to clearly maintain that the covenants God makes with His people are made between a superior and a subordinate, not between two equal parties. So, that word was rejected.

They came back to the word *diathēkē* because in its original use, before it developed in the Greek culture as a word for "testament," it had reference to what is called "the disposition for one's self." A *diathēkē* had to do with an individual's disposition of his goods or property for himself; that is, it referred to his sovereign right to determine to whom his estate would be given. That was an element that blended well with the Hebrew concept, because God chooses to give promises to whomever He will give those promises. He made a covenant with Abraham that He did not make with Hammurabi. He chose the Jews; He did not choose the Philistines. He entered a covenant relationship with them and said, "I will walk among you and be your God, and you shall be My people" (Lev. 26:12). That was not a choice the Israelites made, but one that God made. So, even though in the Greek word *diathēkē* there is some confusion about its content in the Greek culture, it, more than any word in the language, carries the notion of something beyond an agreement that is so important to our understanding of the Hebrew notion of covenant. As we look at the various covenants of Scripture, I hope that it will become clearer how important this is for our understanding of the structure of divine revelation.

DISTINGUISHING THE COVENANTS

As I mentioned, we use the language "Old Testament" and "New Testament," and "old covenant" and "new covenant." I used to tease my students and ask, "Who's the most important prophet in the Old Testament?" They would say, "Elijah," "Isaiah," "Jeremiah," "Ezekiel," or "Daniel." Then I would say, "No, no, the greatest prophet in the Old Testament is John the Baptist." They were always outraged. They would respond, "What do you mean? He's in the New Testament!" That was the point I wanted to get across. Jesus said, "Assuredly, I say to you, among those born of women there has not risen one greater than John the Baptist" (Matt. 11:11). Yes, we read of the birth of John the Baptist in the book that we call the New Testament. But in terms of the history of redemption, or the economy of God's redemption, the new covenant had not yet been established at the time of John's birth. We read about him in the New Testament, but the period of redemptive history in which

John was born was the old covenant. He belonged to that period of redemptive history.

There are endless debates about when the new covenant period really began. Some people say it began at the time of Jesus' resurrection, and others point to the day of Pentecost. I'm persuaded that the new covenant began in the upper room on the night before Jesus' death, when He changed the significance of the Passover and declared the making of a new covenant in His blood—which He ratified the next day on the cross. So, that's when I think the period of redemptive history that we call the new covenant really began.

However, we can see the confusion, because in our most ordinary use of language, when we talk about the Old Testament and the New Testament, we're not talking about two covenants; we're talking about two collections of books: the Old Testament scriptures and the New Testament scriptures. We're talking about two segments of the biblical canon. In that sense, the use of the word has nothing to do with the concept of a testament or will. When we talk about the old covenant or the new covenant, we're not speaking about the concept of a testament but about a period of time.

The old covenant period of redemption does not cover the whole history of the Old Testament, because the old covenant did not start until the fall. When we refer to the old covenant, we're referring to what God promised after the fall. So, we have to make more distinctions and distinguish between what we call the covenant of creation and the covenant of redemption, and we'll begin to do just that in the next chapter.

CHAPTER 1

STUDY GUIDE

INTRODUCTION

The word *covenant* gets tossed around a lot—especially in Reformed circles. The difficulty lies in the fact that "covenant" remains a hard concept to comprehend. Yet many theologians treat it as a central interpretive principle of Scripture and Israel's history. Is it really all that important? Do we really miss something in Scripture if we leave the study of biblical covenants up to the scholars? The answer is a resounding "Yes!" In this chapter, Dr. R. C. Sproul expounds on the meaning of "covenant" and its development in the early history of translation.

SCRIPTURE READINGS

Genesis 21:27; 26:28; 31:44; Judges 2:1–2; Ezra 10:3; Proverbs 2:16–17; Ezekiel 16:8; Malachi 2:14

LEARNING OBJECTIVE

To understand the meaning of the word *covenant* as it relates to God's covenant with humanity.

QUOTATION

Know therefore that the LORD your God is God, the faithful God who keeps covenant and steadfast love with those who love him and keep his command- ments, to a thousand generations.

—Deuteronomy 7:9

OUTLINE

I. Biblical Words

A. *Berîyth*: This Hebrew word is translated into English as "covenant." When used to describe God's covenant with man, it simply refers to an agreement that rests on God's sovereignty with divine sanction.

B. *Diathēkē*: The scholars who translated the Old Testament into Greek (ca. 250 BC) used this Greek word meaning "testament" for the Hebrew word *berîyth*. While not an equivalent meaning, "testament" does denote the notion that God sovereignly covenants with whomever He wills. This translation has led to some confusion. A "testament" can be changed anytime by the testator. He or she can disinherit those previously in the testament. But God's testament is steadfast. Another inadequacy of this word *testament* comes from the fact that the benefits of a testament come *after* the death of the testator—not before.

C. *Sunkatathesis:* This Greek word was rejected because it denoted more of a mutual commitment, purpose, origin, and obligation. The Bible depicts God as the One who is utterly faithful to the covenant, needing to rely on no one for its completion.

D. We must keep in mind that the "Testaments" of the Old and New are literary divisions, and we must not confuse that use of "testament" with the biblical concept of "covenant." Who was the greatest prophet of the Old Testament? Is his story found within the pages of the Old Testament?

E. Our story about the old covenant begins with the fall of humanity. But was there any "arrangement" between God and Adam before he fell? The next three lectures will explore this aspect of biblical covenants.

STUDY QUESTIONS

1. *Beriyth* is the Hebrew word for "_____" in English.
    a. Thanksgiving
    b. Faithfulness
    c. Covenant
    d. None of the above

2. What English word is translated from the Greek word *diathēkē*?
    a. Mutual commitment
    b. Mutual purpose
    c. Testament
    d. None of the above

3. God is depicted in Scripture as One who is utterly faithful to the covenant, _____.
    a. Yet needing to rely on a person's sanction to enact the covenant
    b. Needing to rely on no one for its completion
    c. Needing only to start it, while relying on us to finish it
    d. None of the above

4. Who was the greatest prophet of the Old Testament?
    a. Isaiah
    b. John the Baptist
    c. Jeremiah
    d. None of the above

5. The "Old Testament" refers to _____.

    a. The Mosaic covenant

    b. The Abrahamic covenant

    c. The Davidic covenant

    d. The compilation of ancient writings from Genesis to Malachi

6. Our story about the old covenant begins with _____.

    a. The covenant of redemption

    b. The rise of David to the throne

    c. Noah's flood

    d. The fall of humanity

DISCUSSION GUIDE

1. Was the relationship Adam enjoyed in the garden with God necessary because of Adam's being created? Or was it a gracious privilege? What parameters did God choose to define that relationship (*berîyth, diathēkē*)?

2. Why are the various arrangements God has made with humanity properly called "covenants"?

3. What are some of the elements of a biblical covenant as described in this lecture?

4. Do you think that the Bible itself warrants reading it in a covenantal framework, or do you think this has been wrongfully superimposed upon the Scriptures? Defend your answer biblically.

5. Define the words *berîyth* and *diathēkē*, and how the latter is more appropriate than *sunkatathesis* when describing the covenant between God and humanity.

SUGGESTED READING FOR FURTHER STUDY

Robertson, O. Palmer. *The Christ of the Covenants,* pp. 27–53

Vos, Geerhardus. *Biblical Theology: Old and New Testaments,* pp. 19–26

2

THE COVENANT
OF REDEMPTION

The biblical revelation that we encounter in Scripture is progressive; that is, there is a gradual unfolding of God's revelation. He does not give it all to us in the book of Genesis. But as history moves through time, God gives more and more revelation of Himself and of His plan of redemption. That continuing, progressive revelation is not corrective. It is not the case that the newest revelation corrects the old; God does not need to be corrected. Rather, He augments or adds additional content to His revelation as time passes. And again, the basic structure that carries that progression is the structure of covenant.

When was the first covenant made? In theology, we find evidence of a covenant that is not reported directly in Scripture. Rather, it is deduced from certain inferences drawn from Scripture, particularly

New Testament passages that deal with our understanding of the mission and the purpose and work of Jesus. A few years ago, I preached through the gospel of John, and I was reminded again how much of that book is a record of the controversies that Jesus had with the Jewish authorities of His day. Many of the debates between Jesus and the Pharisees or Jesus and the scribes had to do with His origin and the basis of His authority. And again and again in the gospel of John, Jesus said that He was sent from the Father, that He is the supreme missionary of God. A missionary is someone who is sent and authorized by the person or group that sends him. Christ constantly referred back to His origin, not to the place of His birth in Bethlehem, but to heaven, from whence He was sent to earth by the Father and authorized by the Father to speak the Father's word.

If we understand the fact that Jesus was sent and authorized by the Father, we understand something of what went on before God created the world, before God created Adam and Eve, before there was any kind of probation in the garden of Eden. We talk in the first instance not about a covenant that God makes with us, but a covenant that was forged within the triune Godhead itself. In theological parlance, we call this the covenant of redemption. It speaks to us about an agreement that has existed from all eternity among the persons of the Godhead with regard to God's plan of redemption.

A UNITY OF PURPOSE

When I was in graduate school in the 1960s, a controversy was brewing among German theologians on the Continent. They were arguing that the ministry of Jesus was impelled by His desire to overcome the vengeful, wrathful inclinations of the Old Testament God. This idea went all the way back to the heresy of Marcion (ca. AD 85–160) in the early church, who expunged all references in the New Testament to God as the Father of Jesus, because he thought that there was a basic incompatibility between Christ and the God of the Old Testament. There are still many people who hold this basic idea. They say, "Well, I like the Jesus of the New Testament; it's that Old Testament God I can't stomach; He's such a vengeful God." So, the idea arose in German theology that Christ came in an effort to change God's mind, to convince Him to relent from His purpose and plan to judge people and expose them to His wrath. Basically, then, the salvific work of Christ had to do with His persuading the Father to ease up, as it were. So, Christ reveals to us mercy, whereas the Father was all judgment.

I cannot think of anything that is more distortive of the biblical portrait of both God the Father and God the Son than this kind of understanding. The concept behind the covenant of redemption is that the plan of salvation is conceived in the Godhead, and, in a sense, it is the Father's plan. It is He who sends the Son into the world. The Son does not come on His own initiative. In fact, Jesus said, "Most assuredly, I say to you, the Son can do nothing of Himself, but what He sees the Father do; for whatever He does, the Son also does in like manner" (John 5:19). So, the Son came from heaven to do the will of the Father in this world because the two of them, God the Father and God the Son, are in perfect agreement from all eternity about the mission that the Son will fulfill in this world. The Father and the Son are one in their eternal purpose—and we could add the Holy Spirit, for He also is in complete agreement with the Father and the Son regarding God's plan of redemption.

So, we believe that there was a covenant made among the persons of the Godhead (Father, Son, and Holy Spirit) prior to creation. We often say that in the economy of redemption, the Father sends the Son into the world to redeem His people; the Son accomplishes that redemption by His work of obedience; and the Holy Spirit then applies the work of Christ to the people of God. The Spirit illumines the Word of God for us, regenerates our spirit to new life, draws us to the Son, and reconciles us to the Father. Thus, in biblical categories, redemption is a Trinitarian work from beginning to end.

The great truth that rests on the concept of the covenant of redemption is that redemption was not an afterthought in the plan of God. It was not God's Plan B, which He was forced to come up with to correct the mess humanity made out of creation. No, before He created the world, God had an eternal purpose of redemption, a plan for redeeming His people in this world, and all three persons of the Trinity were in complete agreement about it. Thus, the idea of covenant is rooted and grounded in the character of God Himself.

ACTIVE AND PASSIVE OBEDIENCE

When we think about the outworking of the covenant of redemption, both historic Reformed theology and Protestant theology in general make a distinction with respect to the obedience of the second person of the Trinity, Jesus Christ. It is a distinction between His perfect active obedience and His perfect passive obedience.

The active obedience of Christ has to do with His work as the second Adam, willingly placing Himself under the requirements of the law, taking upon Himself the responsibility to keep the law on our behalf, and actively obeying every commandment that God requires from human beings. Jesus manifested His active obedience in that confusing instance when He came to John the Baptist to be baptized along with all the people of Judea, for John had called them to come and be baptized as a sign of cleansing from sin. When John saw Jesus, he declared Him to be the Lamb of God who was going to take away the sin of the world (John 1:29), meaning He was a Lamb without blemish. But then Jesus asked to be baptized. John was aghast. He said, "Wait a minute. I just told everyone that You're the Lamb of God. You are without sin. You should be baptizing me. I can't baptize You—You're not a sinner" (see Matt. 3:13–14). What did Jesus say? "Permit it to be so now, for thus it is fitting for us to fulfill all righteousness" (Matt. 3:15). He did not go into a lengthy discourse on why He wanted John the Baptist to baptize Him. He essentially pulled rank on John and said, "Just baptize Me; it has to be done."

But why did it have to be done? If Jesus was going to be the second Adam, the new representative of the people, He had to fulfill in His own person all of the obligations that God had imposed on His people. In a real sense, He became the incarnation of Israel, and He had to do everything that the law required of those people, including undergoing baptism as commanded by God's prophet, John the Baptist. So, He actively pursued obedience. His food was to do the will of the Father (John 4:34).

By contrast, we also speak of Jesus' passive obedience. We cannot make this an absolute distinction, because Jesus actively submitted Himself to passive acceptance of the requirements of the Father, and this had to do with His suffering. His active obedience is that obedience by which He achieved perfect righteousness and thereby merited redemption for His people. So, He supplied us with the righteousness we need. At the same time, He took upon Himself the punishments that we deserve by submitting Himself to the judgment of God. You can see this most clearly in His struggle in the garden of Gethsemane, when Jesus had the cup of divine wrath set before Him, the cup of God's judgment. He groaned and said, "O My Father, if it is possible, let this cup pass from Me; nevertheless, not as I will, but as You will" (Matt. 26:39). Of course, the Father required Him to drink the cup and to embrace the cross. At that point, Christ was passive. He was receiving in Himself the curse of the old covenant. He was receiving in Himself the punishment of God on behalf of His people.

And all of this was agreed upon in eternity before Christ ever became flesh and dwelled among us. He agreed to do the work necessary for our redemption. That's why we call it the covenant of redemption between the Father and the Son, and, by extension, the Holy Spirit.

CHAPTER 2

STUDY GUIDE

INTRODUCTION

Knowing God means knowing that He is and will be utterly faithful to His covenant on our behalf. Scripture does not give us the full details of the plan that took place between the triune Godhead in the past. But it does disclose the manifestation of that covenant in time—from God's redemptive work through the nation of Israel in the stories of the Old Testament to the culminating appearance of the God-man, Jesus the Christ. In this chapter, Dr. R. C. Sproul explores the covenantal theme in Scripture and the foundational intra-Trinitarian covenant of redemption.

SCRIPTURE READINGS

Psalm 89:3–4; Isaiah 42:5–9; 53:10–12; Luke 22:28–30; John 10:18; 17:4–5

LEARNING OBJECTIVES

1. To understand the centrality of the covenantal theme in Scripture.
2. To be able to articulate what the covenant of redemption is and how it relates to God's work of reconciling His creation to Himself.

QUOTATION

And Peter said to them, "Repent and be baptized every one of you in the name of Jesus Christ for the forgiveness of your sins, and you will receive the gift of the Holy Spirit. For the promise is for you and for your children and for all who are far off, everyone whom the Lord our God calls to himself."

—Acts 2:38–39

OUTLINE

I. Scriptural Theme: Covenant

A. The whole concept of "covenant" is basic to understanding Scripture. We can go so far as to say that God's work with and in creation is couched in covenantal terms.

B. One major principle of this Scriptural theme is that revelation is progressive. That is, each subsequent revelation from God is not a corrective on what He has previously said; rather, each revelation augments or adds content to the previous one.

C. The word *covenant* does not simply mean "agreement." We must not allow our own Western conceptions of "covenant" to dictate the Scriptural meaning. But many of our own conceptions do have elements found in the biblical covenants (e.g., "promises").

D. Biblical covenants have a more profound religiosity inherent in them. They are wrought by divine sanction, and depict an integral relationship between promises and fulfillments (i.e., God *always* fulfills His word).

E. Thus, the Christian is to walk by faith—a faith that is nothing less than being fully persuaded of the promises of God, which will lead us in gratitude to live in covenant with Him.

F. This, of course, is impossible to do without His grace. While we have not seen or heard God, His Word has been given for this reason: to attest to His covenant faithfulness.

II. The Covenant of Redemption

A. Much controversy surrounded Jesus during His lifetime. From whence did He come?

B. By whose authority? What was His origin? The answers to these questions bear on this first covenant among the Godhead.

C. Christ Jesus did not come to change what God had revealed prior to His arrival, or as is commonly misunderstood, to show mercy in contradistinction to the Old Testament "God of wrath."

D. All along, Jesus was doing the will of His Father. They were one in their eternal purpose. He did nothing on His own initiative, but came because of an intra-Trinitarian covenant—a covenant that was not "Plan B."

E. In this covenant, the Father sent the Son, the Son accomplished the plan, and the Spirit applied the Son's accomplished work to the people of the triune God.

F. Typically, Jesus' work in redemption is discussed in two ways:

1. *Perfect Active Obedience:* Jesus actively and willfully put Himself under the law of God (e.g., He was baptized just as sinners in need of cleansing were to do). Jesus needed to accomplish all that God required Israel to do. Thus, He became the embodiment of Israel. And as the Israel of God, He achieved perfect righteousness and earned redemption for His people.

2. *Perfect Passive Obedience:* This work Jesus did on the cross. He subjugated Himself to the curses of the covenant, to the judgment and wrath of the Father, on behalf of His people.

STUDY QUESTIONS

1. Each subsequent covenant revealed in Scripture corrects the problems with God's previous plan.

> a. True
>
> b. False
>
> c. Both true and false
>
> d. I don't know.

2. The covenant of redemption describes _____.

> a. The intra-Trinitarian agreement to redeem a people for God's glory
>
> b. The intra-Trinitarian agreement to damn a people for God's glory
>
> c. Both a and b
>
> d. None of the above

3. The covenant of redemption was God's _____.

> a. Response to what had taken Him by surprise: the fall of humanity
>
> b. Response to the Israelite nation's failure to keep the covenant of works

c. Plan to provide salvation for sinners via the death of Jesus on the cross

d. None of the above

4. Which of the following best describes the "active obedience" of Jesus?

    a. The passion (death and resurrection)

    b. Jesus put Himself under the law of God and perfectly abided in it.

    c. Jesus put Himself under the law of God and abolished all of it.

    d. All of the above

5. Much of the Bible is couched in _____ terms.

    a. Scientific

    b. Covenantal

    c. Both a and b

    d. None of the above

6. By whose authority did Jesus come to earth?

    a. His own

    b. The Father's

    c. The Holy Spirit's

    d. All of the above

DISCUSSION GUIDE

1. According to this chapter and the previous chapter, what are the roles of the Father, Son, and the Holy Spirit in the covenant of redemption? Are there any Scripture passages that inform your answer?

2. Read John 17:18–19 and Galatians 4:4. How do these contribute to our understanding of an agreement between the Godhead before creation?

3. Explain how the covenant of redemption relates to the salvation of sinners in time.

4. Are there any portions of Scripture that come to mind when discussing God's definite plan for His work of redemption?

5. Is the covenant of redemption inconsistent with the idea that we have the free will to choose according to our desires? Explain your answer.

6. In the covenant of redemption, did the Father agree to call out classes (i.e., a certain group of people) or individuals into the service of the Son?

7. Can you define or describe any faulty views that you may have heard or read on this subject? How would you respond to the person who argues that the idea of this covenant is pure speculation?

8. In what sense is Jesus the Son subordinate to God the Father?

9. What portions of Scripture show that Jesus voluntarily took His task upon Himself (for starters, John 10:18; Phil. 2:8)?

SUGGESTED READING FOR FURTHER STUDY

Robertson, O. Palmer. *The Christ of the Covenants,* pp. 3–25, 91–92

3

THE CREATION COVENANT (PART 1)

The first covenant God made with humanity is known by various names. Sometimes it is referred to simply as "the Adamic covenant." At other times, it is called "the creation covenant." Finally, it is sometimes known by the controversial designation "the covenant of works."

The first covenant is called the Adamic covenant for an obvious reason: it was made with Adam. However, we must remember that the name *Adam* means "man" in the generic sense, mankind. The Bible confirms, particularly in the New Testament, that when God made this covenant, it was not simply between God and a particular historical individual. Rather, Adam represented the whole of humanity. That's very important for our understanding of the history of redemption, because Adam failed as our representative. So, when Christ came into the world, one of the responsibilities the Father gave to Him was to be the "last Adam" (1 Cor. 15:45). We see this contrast mentioned several times in the New Testament. For instance, Paul wrote, "For since by man came death, by Man also came the resurrection of the dead" (1 Cor. 15:21). So, the New Testament makes much of the contrast between the original Adam and Christ as the second Adam, because both functioned not as private individuals but as representatives.

Since Adam represented the entire human race in the covenant that God made with him, all human beings who descend from Adam participate in the Adamic covenant. As the children of Adam, we are necessarily involved in a covenant relationship with God. That's a point that is often overlooked and obscured. People say, "Well, I'm not Jewish and I'm not Christian; therefore, I'm in no covenant relationship with God." They sometimes say, "I don't even believe in God, so there's no way I can be in a covenant relationship with Him." However, the biblical view is that all people are in a covenant relationship with God even if they deny it. We cannot escape this covenantal relationship that was forged between God and us in Adam. Paul referred to Adam's representation in his epistle to the Romans, where he told us that we all sin in Adam (5:12), even though we were not there in the garden of Eden when Satan tempted the man and woman.

So, none of us is outside the covenant. The question is whether we are covenant keepers or covenant breakers. We are all one or the other, but none of us is outside of the covenant. The creation covenant was built in to the order of things before the fall, and the stipulations that God gave to Adam in this covenant were, by extension, given to the whole world.

Were those stipulations that God imposed on Adam in this first covenant ever abrogated or nullified? Sometimes people argue that the commands God gave through Moses in the Old Testament do not apply to us anymore, or that the commands of Jesus apply only to Christians. However, there is little room to argue about the commands God instituted in creation. Any law that God instilled in the covenant of creation extends as far as the creation extends. So, since God sanctified marriage in creation, the sanctity of marriage applies to all generations. No culture has the right before God to dispense with the sanctity of marriage and decide couples can simply live together. The church recognizes civil ceremonies of marriage and does not restrict marriage to the church, giving the state the right to regulate marriage because of the conviction that marriage is given not just to Jews or Christians, but to all human beings. It is an estate that God blesses and sanctifies for the entire human race. It's built into creation. That's why ethical issues that touch on the nature of the family, sexual relationships, and marriage transcend contemporary cultural considerations. These things are rooted and grounded in creation, so they can never be treated as a matter of custom.

CUSTOM AND PRINCIPLE

In my book *Knowing Scripture*, I included a chapter on the difficult interpretive question of custom and principle. We read certain admonitions and exhortations in the Bible, and we ask, "Are these things binding on Christians of all places and all times, or were these simply contemporary customs of a particular culture or era, intended to pass away with that culture or era?"

We know that certain things are given to cultural mutations. For example, when we give our tithes, we do not give God shekels. The principle that we are to be stewards of our property and to support the work of the kingdom of God remains intact, but the particular form of currency that we use changes from culture to culture and from generation to generation.

Also, certain things are determined by culture. The Bible calls Christians in every place and in all generations to dress with modesty. But what is modest in one culture might be considered provocative and obscene in another. If we in the West dressed in the scanty fashion of some of the primitive tribes in the world, it would be scandalous. So, there are differences in the way in which people dress from one generation and one culture to another. That's something that changes; it's fluid. For this reason, we don't require that people wear robes and sandals in twenty-first-century Western culture simply because that's what Jesus wore. Dress is a matter of custom. The principle has to do with that which transcends local customs and applies to all Christians everywhere and at every time.

Sometimes it's very simple to understand the difference between a principle and a custom. Take the example of Christ's command to His disciples to go out but not to take sandals with them (Matt. 10:10). Does that mean that we have a universal mandate from Christ to always do evangelism in our bare feet? Of course not. The way in which people took care of their feet in the first century differs from the way we do it in our contemporary cultures. But not all issues are so simple. Consider the issue of the structure of authority in the home or in the marriage. Is the idea of male headship in the house a matter of custom or a matter of principle? That question is fiercely debated in our own day.

Let's think about a related question: Paul's requirement that women cover their heads in worship (1 Cor. 11:4–6). Almost no one does that today, largely because it is considered to be a cultural command. If you get ten commentaries on 1 Corinthians, you will get ten different opinions about what Paul expected, but almost every one of them will point out that at the time Paul wrote 1 Corinthians, the town of Corinth was known for its immorality and sexuality, and a prostitute could be identified because she walked around with an uncovered head. Thus, it is said, Paul was concerned about the decorum of the Christian community; that is, he didn't want the Christian women of Corinth to appear to be prostitutes, so he told them to cover their heads.

That's the explanation we read in commentary after commentary. But I have a problem with that. It is simply this: Paul never said in 1 Corinthians that the reason he wanted the women to cover their heads was so that they wouldn't look like prostitutes. If the Apostle gave an admonition that is puzzling to us, I think it's a legitimate work of the biblical interpreter to examine the "life situation" in which the text was written.

I think it helps us understand the Bible to read what the contemporary culture was like and to ask ourselves, "How did people in the first century understand this text or this admonition?" That's a legitimate approach to biblical interpretation. However, since the Apostle gave a reason for his injunction, it is not legitimate to dismiss his reason and replace it with a speculative rationale that we draw from our study of the contemporary culture.

In 1 Corinthians, Paul not only said that the women should cover their heads, but also gave a reason. The reason is that covering the head is a sign of the subordination of the wife to the husband in the family (11:6–10). Furthermore, when Paul gave this command, he did not appeal to the local culture in Corinth; he appealed to creation (vv. 8–9).

So, we need to be very careful before dismissing a mandate of God as a local custom that is not binding upon us. If we must err between custom and principle, there's a biblical principle to teach us how to err—the principle that "whatever is not from faith is sin" (Rom. 14:23). In other words, the burden of proof when we come to a mandate in Scripture is always upon those who would say it's a custom rather than those who would say it's a principle. If the Bible tells me to do something that appears to be a custom, and I'm too scrupulous and I treat a custom as a principle, all I'm doing is being overscrupulous. But if I take a principle that God has established for His people and dismiss it as a mere custom, I am guilty of subverting the very law of God. And if we find something that is rooted in creation, that's the last thing that we should treat as a custom, because if anything transcends local considerations, it is that principle that is established in creation, because such principles are binding as long as creation endures.

THE COVENANT OF WORKS

As I mentioned above, the designation for God's covenant with Adam that is most controversial is "the covenant of works." In historic Reformed theology particularly, a distinction is made between what is called the covenant of works and the covenant of grace. The Westminster Confession of Faith, a seventeenth-century Reformed document, says, "The distance between God and the creature is so great, that although reasonable creatures do owe obedience unto Him as their Creator, yet they could never have any fruition of Him as their blessedness and reward, but by some voluntary condescension on God's part, which He hath been pleased to express by way of covenant." Then it adds, "The first covenant made with man was a covenant of works, wherein life was promised to Adam; and in him to his posterity, upon condition of perfect and personal obedience" (7.1–2).[1]

Here's where the confusion comes in. In the first section, the framers of the Westminster Confession were expressing the idea that we do not have a creational entitlement program. When God made us out of the dust, He was under no obligation to give us prosperity, good health, or eternal life. The creature cannot say to the Creator, "You must do this and that for me." Any benefit that we receive from the Creator comes not out of some divine necessity or some kind of external law that is imposed upon God by the nature of things. Instead, any benefit that we get as creatures comes from God's personal disposition.

In the first chapter, I discussed how the scholars who translated the Hebrew scriptures into Greek settled on the Greek word *diathēkē* to translate the Hebrew word for "covenant," *berîyth*. I mentioned that *diathēkē* ultimately was chosen because it had the element of sovereign disposition. That's very important, because we have been conditioned in modern culture to think in terms of entitlement programs. We think that if we don't get certain things, there's some miscarriage of justice. We think that the state owes us a college education. It owes us a certain wage level. It owes us this, and it owes us that. Where do we get that idea? Who said that any government ever owed its people anything other than just rule?

In the end, I believe that's just the way we are as creatures. Unfortunately, we let that tendency influence our thinking with respect to how God relates to us. God does not owe us anything. Any blessing that He gives to us comes from Him voluntarily, by His grace. And that principle is firmly set forth in the Westminster Confession: "The distance between God and the creature is so great, that although reasonable creatures do owe obedience unto Him as their Creator, yet they could never have any fruition of Him as their blessedness and reward, but by some voluntary condescension on God's part, which He hath been pleased to express by way of covenant."[2]

This truth is enmeshed in the very nature of things because "it is He who has made us, and not we ourselves" (Ps. 100:3b). We owe Him. We are debtors to Him for our very existence. We owe Him everything; He owes us nothing. Yet, He blesses us richly, and as the confession says, our participation in blessedness comes from the "voluntary condescension on God's part, which He hath been pleased to express by way of covenant."

Doesn't that mean that the first covenant is not a covenant of works but a covenant of grace? No, the distinction between the covenant of works and the covenant of grace is not intended to say that. The point of the distinction between the covenant of works and the covenant of grace is what conditions God imposes upon those of us who are in covenant with Him for our experience of its benefits.

We all agree, I think, that for God to enter into a covenant with us at all is gracious. Because of that point, there are some people who object to the distinction between the covenant of works and the covenant of grace. They think that it obscures the reality that any covenant that we have with God is only by His grace. It is gracious that He would make any kind of a covenant with us in the first place. This distinction needs further examination, and we will turn to that in the next chapter.

CHAPTER 3

STUDY GUIDE

INTRODUCTION

The first covenant made between God and humanity took place in the garden of Eden. It has been called many things, and there are as many opinions about it as there are theologians. But essential to our understanding of this first covenant is how it relates to the gracious covenant to follow. Some scholars contend that there just is no Scriptural warrant for calling this agreement in the garden a "covenant." Dr. R. C. Sproul contends otherwise, for a basic understanding of this agreement as a covenant is necessary if we are to understand the finished work of the living Savior.

In this chapter, Dr. Sproul discusses and explains the various names given to this covenant.

SCRIPTURE READINGS

Genesis 2:17; Romans 5:12–21; 10:5; Galatians 3:10–14

LEARNING OBJECTIVE

To recognize and understand the various names for God's covenant with humanity in the garden of Eden.

QUOTATIONS

So God created man in his own image, in the image of God he created him; male and female he created them.... And God blessed them. And God said to them, "Be fruitful and multiply and fill the earth and subdue it, and have dominion over the fish of the sea and over the birds of the heavens and over every living thing that moves on the earth."

—Genesis 1:27–28

The first covenant made with man was a covenant of works, wherein life was promised to Adam; and in him to his posterity, upon condition of perfect and personal obedience.

—The Westminster Confession of Faith, 7.2

OUTLINE

I. The First Covenant with Humanity

A. This covenant is known by various names for different reasons.

1. *Adamic covenant*: The word *adam* actually means "mankind." God made a covenant not just with the historical person Adam, but with those whom he represented. This concept is most succinctly articulated in Paul's letter to the Romans, wherein the author made much ado about the "first" and "second" Adam. They both worked as representatives of the entire human race. This means that those who descended from Adam are by necessity in a covenant relationship with God. It cannot be escaped or denied. Ethnicity makes no difference whatsoever. Thus, the big question is this: Are we covenant breakers or covenant keepers? All of humanity falls into one camp or the other.

2. *Creation covenant*: It is called thus because covenantal-type sanctions were imposed upon the entire created order. None of these have ever been abrogated. Any divine sanction put into effect at creation extends as far as

creation itself. One example of this would be the sanctity of marriage. We recognize marriage in the civilized world because marriage is for *all* humanity—not just for the ancient Israelites or Christians.

a) If rooted or grounded in the act of creation, a law cannot be reduced to cultural custom.

b) In order to best understand certain portions of Scripture, we need to grasp the difference between "customs" and "principles." Customs change, but the overarching principles do not. For example, with respect to the way we dress: Do women wear hats or not? Must we evangelize without shoes on like Jesus instructed His disciples to do? Is male headship in the home custom or principle?

3. *Covenant of works:* This third common name for the first covenant God made with humanity is by far the most controversial. Why? Because many see it as an intrusion of systematic theology onto biblical theology. But the critic should remember that any time the Bible's main themes are being summarized systematic theology is taking place. Both approaches to theology have proved equally helpful to the church.

a) In Reformed theology in general, and the Westminster Confession of Faith in particular, a distinction is made between the covenant of works and the covenant of grace: any benefit the creature gets comes by God's own personal disposition. The creature is not entitled to anything; God owes us nothing, but He gives voluntarily (see WCF 7.1). We therefore owe Him everything; that is, we owe Him our very existence. God, in the sheer act of communicating with His creatures, must condescend to them. This condescension God accommodates to our human understanding, and therefore takes the shape of a covenant. Our next chapter will cover the distinctions between the covenant of works and the covenant of grace.

STUDY QUESTIONS

1. Which of the following is *not* a name for the covenant between Adam and his Creator?

    a. The Adamic covenant

    b. The covenant of works

    c. The covenant of redemption

    d. The creation covenant

2. The word *adam* actually means "_____."

    a. Male

    b. Mankind

    c. Clay

    d. One

3. The first covenant God made with humanity is often called "the Adamic covenant" because _____.

    a. That was the first man's name, Adam

    b. The covenant was made with Adam and the entire race he represented

    c. Adam took the initiative in making this covenant with God

    d. None of the above

4. The first covenant God made outside of Himself is often called "the creation covenant" because _____.

    a. It was made with the first man

    b. Covenantal-type sanctions were imposed upon only the animal kingdom

    c. God "created" a covenant with Adam and Eve

    d. Covenantal-type sanctions were imposed upon the entire created order

5. The main difference between customs and principles is that _____.

    a. There is no difference

    b. Customs change, but the overarching principles do not

    c. Principles change, but the overarching customs do not

    d. None of the above

6. The covenant of works (by far the most controversial name for the first covenant God made with humanity) is _____.

     a. Not to be distinguished from the covenant of grace

     b. A result of systematizing biblical theology

     c. Both a and b

     d. None of the above

DISCUSSION GUIDE

1. Read Romans 5:12–21. What might be the biblical reasons for calling the covenant between God and Adam "Adamic"?

2. How does a clear understanding of the Adamic covenant help us follow the gist of Paul's argument in 1 Corinthians 15:12–28?

3. Read Genesis 1–2. What parts of this passage accentuate elements emphasized in the "creation covenant"?

4. Using Scripture, describe some of the covenantal-type sanctions that God imposed upon His created order.

5. What are your opinions about customs and principles, and how do they relate to the issues discussed in this chapter?

6. Explain why the covenant of works must be considered a gracious condescension on the part of God.

7. Are any of the various names for this covenant better than the others? Why or why not? Do you think systematic theology imposes unbiblical principles upon the sacred text?

SUGGESTED READING FOR FURTHER STUDY

Robertson, O. Palmer. *The Christ of the Covenants,* pp. 67–74

NOTES

1. "Of God's Covenant with Man," *The Westminster Confession of Faith,* Center for Reformed Theology and Apologetics, accessed February 22, 2013, http://www.reformed.org/documents/wcf_with_proofs/.
2. "Of God's Covenant with Man," *The Westminster Confession of Faith,* Center for Reformed Theology and Apologetics, accessed February 22, 2013, http://www.reformed.org/documents/wcf_with_proofs/.

4

THE CREATION COVENANT (PART 2)

As we have been considering the covenants God has made with humanity, we have used terms such as "old covenant" and "new covenant." In the previous chapter, as we began considering God's first covenant with humanity, we saw that it is variously called "the Adamic covenant," "the creation covenant," or "the covenant of works," as distinct from "the covenant of grace." All these terms produce much confusion.

Historically, Reformed theology has viewed the unfolding of redemptive history in this manner: first there was the covenant of works and then the covenant of grace, and under the covenant of grace are the old covenant and the new covenant. That is, the distinction between the old covenant and the new covenant is an economic distinction or a difference in the historical dispensation, the way in which God worked out the covenant of grace. The old covenant has reference to the original unfolding of the covenant of grace that we read about primarily in the Old Testament, and then we move to the new covenant, which is also a manifestation of the covenant of grace. However, even though we make these distinctions, there remains a connection between the covenant of works and the new covenant.

The basic difference is this: in the covenant of works, the human race was put on probation and promised life eternal on the condition of obedience to the commands of God. When humanity failed to keep that covenant, God, in His grace, made a new covenant based on that grace. The terms of the covenant of works were not set aside but were fulfilled in a different manner, as I trust we will be able to see. But before we can do that, we have to establish that there was such a thing as the covenant of works and see how we are to understand it in creation.

People frequently ask, "What was the moral state of Adam and Eve before the fall? Were they perfect? Were they perfectly righteous? What was their condition?" This issue has sparked an enormous amount of debate historically. To some degree, the question has to do with what it means that Adam and Eve were made in the image of God. Genesis tells us: "Then God said, 'Let Us make man in Our image, according to Our likeness; let them have dominion over the fish of the sea, over the birds of the air, and over the cattle, over all the earth and over every creeping thing that creeps on the earth.' So God created man in His own image; in the image of God He created him; male and female He created them" (Gen. 1:26–27). Notice here that two words are used to convey the manner in which God made humanity: *image* and *likeness*. Is the Genesis account referring to two separate things here, or are these two words both describing the same thing? The Roman Catholic Church historically has distinguished between *image* and *likeness*, and historic Protestantism has not. Historic Protestantism has seen *image* and *likeness* as both referring to the same thing—the way in which there is some similitude between the Creator and the creature.

So, if Adam and Eve were made in the image of God, what happened to their condition and their status with God after the fall? Is humanity still made in the image of God? The Scriptures make it clear that even though we were plunged into a ruinous state of corruption by the fall of Adam and Eve, that fall did not completely destroy the image of God in us. Yet it is difficult to pinpoint how marred the image is, and theologians have wrestled with this over the ages.

Perhaps the deepest insights on this question came from Augustine (AD 354–430). He said that in addition to their basic human nature, Adam and Eve were given a kind of a plus that was not absolutely inherent to their humanity. That is, it was a gift they could lose and still maintain their humanity. This gift is called the gift of original righteousness.

What is the difference between innocence and righteousness? There is no doubt that Adam and Eve in creation were innocent. To be innocent means to be free from any sin or any impurity. Adam and Eve were not guilty creatures at the time God set them in the garden of Eden. They were innocent of sin. However, that is not the same thing as having positive righteousness. Positive righteousness is manifested by actually living in agreement with the commandments of God. Righteousness is established through obedience. So, some say Adam and Eve were only innocent, and there was no added gift of righteousness in the garden before the fall, a gift that was then lost.

We have the tendency to think that in our redemption through the ministry of Christ, the second Adam, we are restored to Paradise because of Christ's obedience. However, that is not the biblical view. If our justification merely put us back into the condition Adam and Eve were in before the fall, we still would not have the positive righteousness necessary to have eternal life. Even Adam and Eve did not have that at the time of the fall. They were innocent, but they had not yet acquired positive righteousness. We know this because God had not yet given them permission to partake of the tree of life.

The point Augustine was most jealous to maintain was this: humanity was created good, but mutably good, not immutably good. Humanity's constituent nature could change for better or worse. That is, in their created state, Adam and Eve could improve their standing before God through their obedience, or they could worsen their status before God through disobedience.

THE TREE OF LIFE

So, the symbolism that we find in the garden of Eden is very important for us in understanding the covenants of works and of grace.

Historically, most biblical Christians, and certainly those in the Reformed faith, have maintained that the state of Adam and Eve in the garden prior to the fall was a state of probation. That is, they were to be judged and evaluated in terms of their obedience or disobedience to the first command God placed upon them. If they obeyed, they would receive access to the tree of life; if they disobeyed, they would suffer the consequences of the curse and of death.

This is so very important because, when we turn to the New Testament and look at the ministry of Christ as the second Adam, we see that Christ wins what Adam failed to win. He wins the tree of life, and He gives that gift to His people, so that we now inherit the benefits that Adam and Eve would have had, had they passed their probation, had they met the terms of the covenant of works. In that case, they would have had eternal life, but they failed and lost it by their sin.

In his classic work *Biblical Theology*, Princeton theologian Geerhardus Vos (1862–1949) examined the Adamic covenant, or the covenant of works, and he found in the biblical account four principles or elements that are important in helping us understand what was going on during this probationary situation. The first is the tree of life. When the Bible describes what it was like in the garden of Eden, it identifies two trees that are distinguished from all the rest of the trees in the garden. There was the tree of life and there was the Tree of Knowledge of Good and Evil (Gen. 2:9). The tree of life, according to Vos, represents the highest possible potency of life for a human being. That's important because Jesus said, "I have come that they may have life, and that they may have it more abundantly"

(John 10:10b). He didn't preach that message at the cemetery. The people to whom He spoke had *bios*, that is, biological life; their vital signs were fine; they were alive and well. But they lacked a special kind of life, that which the Greek calls *zoe*, that life that Christ came to give, which is a higher order of life than anyone was enjoying at that time. Of course, when we get to heaven, we will not be restored simply to the biological state that Adam had. Instead, we are going to be elevated to a higher level of life, one that is eternal and in which there is no sin, no sorrow, no death, no suffering. That is what the new Adam, the second Adam, came to do for us—to provide for us what Adam and Eve failed to provide for us: the tree of life.

We see this clearly in the New Testament. In Revelation 2, Jesus addressed the seven churches of Asia Minor. When He addressed the church of Ephesus and gave His evaluation of the pattern of behavior of that church, He said: "He who has an ear, let him hear what the Spirit says to the churches. To him who overcomes I will give to eat from the tree of life, which is in the midst of the Paradise of God" (v. 7). So, the One who has the authority to dispense the benefits inherent in the tree of life is the new Adam. By His victory, by His obedience, He gains the authority to distribute to His people, those who persevere, the right and the authority to eat from the tree of life.

At the very end of the book of Revelation, we see a description of the glory of the New Jerusalem:

> And he showed me a pure river of water of life,
> clear as crystal, proceeding from the throne of

God and of the Lamb. In the middle of its street, and on either side of the river, was the tree of life, which bore twelve fruits, each tree yielding its fruit every month. The leaves of the tree were for the healing of the nations. And there shall be no more curse, but the throne of God and of the Lamb shall be in it, and His servants shall serve Him. They shall see His face, and His name shall be on their foreheads. There shall be no night there: They need no lamp nor light of the sun, for the Lord God gives them light. And they shall reign forever and ever. (22:1–5)

In this magnificent vision of the final state of the redemption of God's people, we see a river coming from the very throne of God, and on either side of it are trees of life, and their leaves bring healing and the end of all of the dimensions of the curse. That curse, of course, is rooted and grounded in the original fall in Eden.

THE TREE OF KNOWLEDGE

The second principle or element of the covenant of works that Vos identified is the Tree of Knowledge of Good and Evil. In Genesis we read: "The LORD God planted a garden eastward in Eden, and there He put the man whom He had formed. And out of the ground the LORD God made every tree grow that is pleasant to the sight and good for food. The tree of life was also in the midst of the garden, and the tree of the knowledge of good and evil" (2:8–9). Just below, we read: "Then the LORD God took the man and put him in the garden of Eden to tend and keep it. And the LORD God commanded the man, saying, 'Of every tree of the garden you may freely eat; but of the tree of the knowledge of good and evil you shall not eat, for in the day that you eat of it you shall surely die'" (vv. 15–17).

This Tree of Knowledge of Good and Evil certainly represents the principle of probation. The tree of life was not accessible to them; they had not yet participated in it, and that suggests that they were not at the fullest state of life they could potentially enjoy. That, in turn, indicates that they were in a state of testing.

Sometimes we confuse the biblical words *tempt* and *test*. James told us in his epistle: "Let no one say when he is tempted, 'I am tempted by God'; for God cannot be tempted by evil, nor does He Himself tempt anyone. But each one is tempted when he is drawn away by his own desires and enticed" (1:13–14). Usually when we talk about temptation, we mean: "I was almost persuaded to engage in that particular action. I didn't do it, but I was sure tempted to do it." We're talking about an internal condition. On the other hand, we can be tempted externally. If someone comes to us and tries to coax us to participate in sin, we would consider that an external temptation. That's what Satan does all the time. In the garden of Eden, Satan came and tried to persuade Eve to eat from the Tree of Knowledge of Good and Evil. He was operating as the "tempter." But God never tempts anyone in the sense of trying to seduce or entice him or her to sin. Rather, He puts us to the test.

Remember, the Gospels do not tell us that when Christ was driven into the wilderness to be tempted by Satan, that it was the Devil who drove Him there. No, the Spirit drove Jesus into the wilderness in order for Jesus to be tempted by Satan (Matt. 4:1). That is, God was putting His Son to the test. Here again, we see the relationship between the first Adam and the second Adam. Both of them were subjected to the assault of Satan. God put both of them to the test. God subjected Adam and Eve to the temptation of the Serpent, not because God was enticing them, but because He was putting them on trial. This is what we mean when we talk about the probation of Adam and Eve—just as Christ had to be put to the test as the new Adam to be qualified to perform His work of redemption, so Adam and Eve had to be tested with respect to the Tree of Knowledge of Good and Evil. We'll look more closely at the reason why it is called the Tree of Knowledge of Good and Evil in the next chapter.

CHAPTER 4

STUDY GUIDE

INTRODUCTION

Continuing our study of the creation covenant, we turn our attention to the elements of the probationary period established in the garden. Central to this probation were the two trees. What did they symbolize? How are they to be understood? Was the act of eating fruit really all that bad? In this chapter, Dr. R. C. Sproul explains the different aspects of the covenant of works, and begins his discussion on the two trees and their relationship to this period in biblical history.

SCRIPTURE READINGS

Genesis 2:15–17; Leviticus 18:5; Deuteronomy 27:26; Nehemiah 9:29; Matthew 19:16–17; James 2:10

LEARNING OBJECTIVES

1. To understand the distinctions between the covenants of works and grace.
2. To be able to recognize what elements of the garden of Eden narrative have led theologians to discuss it in covenantal terms.

QUOTATIONS

The LORD God took the man and put him in the garden of Eden to work it and keep it. And the LORD God commanded the man, saying, "You may surely eat of every tree of the garden, but of the tree of the knowledge of good and evil you shall not eat, for in the day that you eat of it you shall surely die."

—Genesis 2:15–17

Therefore, as one trespass led to condemnation for all men, so one act of righteousness leads to justification and life for all men. For as by the one man's

> *disobedience the many were made sinners, so by the one man's obedience the many will be made righteous.... Thus it is written, "The first man Adam became a living being"; the last Adam became a life-giving spirit.*

> —Romans 5:18–19; 1 Corinthians 15:45

OUTLINE

I. Elements of the Covenant of Works

A. On the condition of humanity's obedience to the sanctions of this covenant, God would confer the blessings of the covenant (life eternal in His presence).

B. But since humanity failed, God established a covenant of grace that fulfilled the covenant of works without relying on the obedience of fallen humanity.

C. This discussion drives us to understand the nature of humanity in the garden of Eden. The best way to approach this question is by looking at how the postfall image of God in humanity has been shattered (though not utterly destroyed).

D. Bishop Augustine of Hippo wrote that Adam and Eve were endowed with a gift that, if lost, was not essential to their humanity. That is, it did not make them "less than human" when they lost it.

E. Furthermore, in order for Adam to fulfill the covenant of works he needed two things:

    1. Innocence: Humanity was created good, but not without the potential to do bad.

    2. Positive Righteousness: This righteousness, or "utter faithfulness," requires *active* obedience. This perfect obedience would thus entail earning the blessing of the covenant.

F. Adam and Eve, however, were *innocent*, but not *positively righteous*; they were positively unrighteous in their failure of the covenant. It is because of Christ Jesus' positive righteousness that all who believe in Him regain Paradise. But once we believe in Him, if we are then put back under the covenant of works, we would utterly fail again. So, what do we Christians actually regain?

G. Since humanity was in a probationary period in the garden (e.g., "If you eat of the Tree of Knowledge of Good and Evil, then you shall surely die."), Jesus came to do what Adam failed to do, that is, obey perfectly God's commands. Thus in His perfect and positive righteousness, Jesus won or earned the rewards of the covenant and then passes them on to all who would believe in Him.

II. The Two Trees

    A. The Tree of Life: The life inherent in this tree's fruit represents the highest possible potency of life (cf. John

10:10b). In the new heavens and new earth, the life conferred to those who believe in Christ will be a higher life than the one given to Adam and Eve in the garden.

B. It will be greater because believers will be made immutably righteous, that is, they will be unable to sin. Adam and Eve were not given this attribute, as they were merely able not to sin. Only a victorious Adam could dispense such a blessing, giving to those who overcome "the tree of life, which is in the paradise of God" (Rev. 2:7).

C. The Tree of Knowledge of Good and Evil: The knowledge of this tree represents a knowledge that Adam and Eve were not meant to have until God's good timing.

D. God told them not to eat of this tree, for if they did, they would die immediately. This condition represents the period of probation or testing of the covenant of works. While God did not tempt (i.e., entice to sin) Adam and Eve, He did test them.

E. In like manner, Jesus was also put to the test (Mark 1:12–13). The temptation narrative parallels the temptation of Adam, but the second Adam accomplished what the first Adam failed to do.

STUDY QUESTIONS

1. What was the condition that had to be met by Adam in order for God to confer the blessings of the covenant upon him?

a. Adam had to name every animal in the garden.

b. Adam had to obey God's word to not eat of a certain tree.

c. Adam had to attain divinity by obtaining godlike knowledge.

d. None of the above

2. The image of God in humankind has been _____ as a result of the fall.

    a. Utterly destroyed

    b. Shattered

    c. Unaffected

    d. None of the above

3. Adam's "innocence" refers to his _____.

    a. Inability to sin

    b. Inability to not sin

    c. Ability to sin

    d. None of the above

4. "Positive righteousness" is _____.

    a. Becoming like God by obtaining complete knowledge

    b. Doing one's best, which would fulfill the covenant

    c. Perfect active obedience to God's word, which would fulfill the covenant

    d. Both a and b

5. On the final day, believers will be _____.
  a. Able to sin
  b. Unable to not sin
  c. Unable to sin
  d. None of the above

6. What did God say would happen to Adam and Eve if they ate from the Tree of Knowledge of Good and Evil?
  a. "You shall know all things, good and evil."
  b. "You shall not surely die!"
  c. "You shall surely die."
  d. None of the above

DISCUSSION GUIDE

1. Define and describe the several elements of the covenant of works. Use Scripture to support your answer.

2. What was the promise of the covenant of works? What Scripture passages support your answer?

3. Upon what condition was the covenant of works resting? What was the penalty for failing this covenant? Cite those portions of Scripture that support this understanding of the covenant.

4. Why is it so important to Christian theology that Adam and Eve be representatives of the entire human race?

5. According to this chapter, Adam was created innocent, though able to sin. Do we share this in common with him? Why or why not? Support your answer from Scripture.

6. Have you heard anyone argue that we are born morally innocent? How would you respond? How might this notion undermine the work of Christ?

7. In your own words, explain how this agreement in the garden between God and Adam is best defined in covenantal terms. If you do not agree that it is best defined in covenantal terms, then explain why it is not and how we might better define it.

SUGGESTED READING FOR FURTHER STUDY

Robertson, O. Palmer. *The Christ of the Covenants*, pp. 74–87
Vos, Geerhardus. *Biblical Theology: Old and New Testaments*, pp. 27–40

5

THE CREATION COVENANT (PART 3)

Why was the Tree of Knowledge of Good and Evil given such an unusual name? The standard reply is that Adam and Eve did not have an experiential sense of the difference between right and wrong until they experienced the shame that came from their sin. So, the idea was that the knowledge of good and evil could come only through sinning.

However, Adam and Eve were created as moral creatures and were called to discern between right and wrong without first experiencing sin. Likewise, God clearly knows the difference between right and wrong, but He did not have to experience evil to understand that it is evil. So, the idea is not that someone would reap a benefit from the tree only by disobeying the commandment.

The Bible does not explain to us exactly why it was called the Tree of Knowledge of Good and Evil, but I think we get a hint as to the reason for it by virtue of another element that we encounter in the garden: the Serpent who came to our primordial parents as the tempter.

The third chapter of Genesis begins with ominous words. To that point, everything in the creation account had a positive note. God saw everything He had made as good, then judged the totality of it as "very good" (Gen. 1:31). But all that changes as chapter 3 opens. We read there: "Now the serpent was more cunning than any beast of the field which the LORD God had made" (v. 1a). So, the Serpent is introduced as possessing a certain subtlety. And he approached Eve and asked, "Has God indeed said, 'You shall not eat of every tree of the garden'?" (v. 1b).

The Serpent was subtle, not stupid. The Serpent knew very well that God had said to Adam and Eve, "Of every tree of the garden you may freely eat" (2:16), but He then had put certain restrictions in their path. Using those restrictions as the basis of his temptation, Satan said, "Well, did God say you can't eat from all of the trees?" I find an amazing parallel here between the implication of the Serpent and the twentieth-century philosophy of Jean-Paul Sartre, who said that God cannot exist because we exist as human beings. He was saying that the essence of being human is found in freedom, and since we know that we are free, that we are moral agents, then God cannot exist, because if God did exist, humanity would not be autonomous, which means "a law unto oneself."

By contrast, the Bible says that God created us free but not autonomous—in other words, the authority of God always limits our freedom. Only God is a law unto Himself. As our God, He delegates to us all kinds of freedoms, as we see demonstrated in the garden—He gave Adam and Eve freedom to eat from all the trees except one. He grants a high degree of freedom to the creature, but when He places restrictions, He shows that this freedom, however broad it is, nevertheless is limited.

Sartre's argument was that unless we are totally free or autonomous, free to determine for ourselves what is right and what is wrong, then we're not really free at all. And it is fascinating to me that this basically is the same argument the Serpent gave to Eve when he said, "Has God indeed said, 'You shall not eat of every tree of the garden'?"

Every person who has ever been a parent has discovered the subtlety of this argument. Your teenage son comes to you on Monday night and asks: "May I stay out this evening? I want to go to the movies with my buddies. I know it's a school night, but I really want to see this movie." You say, "Okay." Tuesday night he says: "My friends are going out for pizza, and they'd like me to go along. May I go?" Again, you say, "Okay, you may go." Wednesday night he comes home and says, "Dad, may I borrow the car tonight?" You say, "Sure, go ahead, but be home at a reasonable hour." Thursday night he wants to go on a date, and you say, "Okay." Friday night he wants to go to a concert, and once again you give permission. Then, on Saturday night, he wants to go somewhere else with the car, and you say, "Not tonight, Son." What's the normal response a teenager gives at that point? "You never let me do anything." You can say yes five times in a row, but if you finish the sequence with a no, all of a sudden you're a tyrant. You have given your teenager no freedom.

That's the suggestion that the Serpent gave to Eve. "Did God say you couldn't eat from any tree in the garden?" God had said nothing of the sort. In fact, He had said they could eat of nearly all the trees in the garden. But the subtle implication was that by denying one tree to the man and the woman, God might as well have denied all of the trees to them. He suggested that God had not given them freedom but limited their freedom.

TO BE LIKE GOD

After this subtle attack, the Serpent switched quickly to a frontal attack, clearly contradicting what God had said. Eve responded to his initial suggestion by saying, "We may eat the fruit of the trees of the garden; but of the fruit of the tree which is in the midst of the garden, God has said, 'You shall not eat it, nor shall you touch it, lest you die'" (Gen. 3:2–3). The Serpent replied: "You will not surely die. For God knows that in the day you eat of it your eyes will be opened, and you will be like God, knowing good and evil" (vv. 4–5).

Now the temptation, the seduction, is that humanity can be elevated to the very highest level of reality, to the level of God

Himself, to know good and evil as God knows good and evil, presumably to establish the standards of good and evil, to decree what is good, to do what is right in their own eyes. This is, for the creature, the very essence of sin—to do what is right in its own eyes.

That which destroys the covenantal foundation of our relationship to God is the human quest for autonomy. Satan knew this, so he held out to Eve the promise of deification. When Eve and her husband fell into this trap and were seduced by the Serpent, then, of course, the covenant of works, or the covenant of creation, ended in complete disaster. The probation carries with it a punitive element: the promise of death to all who violate the covenant.

It is important for us to understand that the consequence God set forth for disobedience to this covenant was not simply death at some point. He had said, "In the day that you eat of it you shall surely die" (Gen. 2:17). The punishment for breaking the probation of the covenant of creation was not just death but immediate death. But, of course, God did not follow through with that. How should we understand this?

Some people say that Adam and Eve did suffer death in the very moment when they violated the terms of the covenant—spiritual death, from which they could be resurrected only by the power of the Holy Spirit. That is true, but I think more than that is in view in the warning God gave to them. The idea that sinning against God would bring death carries with it the idea of the physical dissolution of the body, biological death, the death that we understand attends every mortal person.

Still, the fact that God did not kill Adam and Eve on the day they sinned does not make God a liar; it simply makes Him gracious. He allowed Adam and Eve, who were now spiritually dead, to continue to live biologically. By postponing their deaths, He provided for them the opportunity of redemption. From the third chapter of Genesis onward, the rest of the Bible is indeed the story of God's work of redemption. All of the future covenants, all of the rest of God's activity with us, is about His purpose of redeeming us from the fall.

The penalty of death that comes upon Adam and Eve is extended to all of their descendants. That is why the New Testament tells us, "by the one man's offense many died" (Rom. 5:15). We all die because we all participate in our original parents' transgression.

THE CURSE FOR SIN

The negative sanction that God imposed upon the human race because of sin is called the curse. After the man and the woman fell, God pronounced His curse on them and on the Serpent (Gen. 3:14–19). The whole idea of the curse in the Bible is the antithesis, the exact opposite, of the divine blessing. It's a malediction by which God condemns people to be separated from Him, sent into the outer darkness to experience the complete loss of the benefits of His nearness.

As part of God's curse, the man was given greatly increased toil in his work. Now the ground was cursed so that when the man used the labor of his hands to produce his livelihood, the ground yielded its fruit reluctantly. Along with useful plants, the ground now sprouted weeds and thorns that made it difficult to farm the land. The effort required to survive became much more severe because of sin. Labor itself is not the curse, because God put Adam and Eve to work in the garden prior to the fall; they were imitating God Himself, who is a working God. Rather, the curse is the difficulty, the frustration, and the frequent futility that accompany our labor.

To the woman God gave the exceeding pain associated with childbirth. She still had the singular privilege of bearing the highest fruit that a human being can possibly bear, which is another human being. Sometimes women don't think that's such a great privilege because of the pain associated with it. Yet, most women will testify that despite the pain, there is no more sanctified moment in human existence than giving birth to a child. Though men cannot identify with that experientially, I think we get some hint of it by being there when the child is born. I will never forget laying eyes on our firstborn child and how the emotions swelled up within me toward my wife. I was in awe that my wife had brought this daughter into the world. It was a fantastic moment that I'll never forget.

The third part of the curse was pronounced on the Serpent. God said that the Serpent would be on his belly in the dust all of his life; and then added the prophetic judgment that the Seed of the woman would crush the Serpent's head. The word *seed* here is not plural; this prophecy indicates one specific individual who would be a descendant of Eve. At some point, this One will come and crush the head of the Serpent, but in the process, the heel of the One who is the Seed of the woman will be bruised. This is known as the *proto-evangelium*, "the first gospel," and the irony is that this first promise of the gospel comes in the middle of God's curse on the Serpent. It anticipates the defeat of Satan by Christ, who would suffer and die as He vanquished the one who seduced Adam and Eve.

Along with these curses and the first promise of redemption, the first act of redemption happened at this time. The immediate response of Adam and Eve to their transgression was a sense of shame connected with their nakedness (Gen. 3:7), whereas previously they had been naked and unashamed (2:25). But when they sinned, they suddenly became aware of their nakedness, and they sought refuge by hiding among the trees.

Desmond Morris, a British zoologist and ethnologist, wrote a bestselling book in the 1960s titled *The Naked Ape*. In it, he looked at humanity not as something specially created in the image of God, but as just one more animal in the animal kingdom. He noted that there are around eighty different species or subspecies of primates in the world, and he included humans as one of those forms. He made a big deal out of the reality that of all of the species of primates in the world, only one of them—in fact, only one animal in the whole animal kingdom—produces artificial coverings for itself. All others wear the clothing that the Creator gave to them, but we alone can hardly bear to be naked. Certainly this was true of Adam and Eve.

So, our first parents felt embarrassment and shame about being naked, and God had pity on them. The very first act of redemption occurred when God stooped down and personally made garments to cover the nakedness of His sinful creatures (Gen. 3:21).

Here we begin to see the covenant of grace beginning to unfold. When human beings failed in obedience to the law of God, God did not just annihilate them. He gave them a promise of future redemption, and He covered their nakedness, which foreshadowed the ultimate covering of our spiritual nakedness that is accomplished by the garments of the righteousness of Christ.

CHAPTER 5

STUDY GUIDE

INTRODUCTION

In this final chapter on the covenant of works, the Tree of Knowledge of Good and Evil is discussed in detail. The tree itself stood as the ultimate test for Adam and Eve: Were they simply going to trust God and His wisdom, or would they reach out in a godless grasp toward that which was not theirs? In this chapter, Dr. R. C. Sproul discusses the forbidden tree and the curse of the fall.

SCRIPTURE READINGS

Genesis 2:15–17; Hosea 6:1–10; Matthew 5:19; Galatians 3:10; James 2:10

LEARNING OBJECTIVES

1. To understand more fully what the Tree of Knowledge of Good and Evil symbolized.
2. To understand the elements of the curse after humanity had fallen.

QUOTATION

For I desire steadfast love and not sacrifice, the knowledge of God rather than burnt offerings. But like Adam they transgressed the covenant; there they dealt faithlessly with me.

—Hosea 6:6–7

OUTLINE

I. The Tree of Knowledge of Good and Evil

A. Typically, the explanation offered for the name of this tree is that Adam and Eve had no experiential knowledge of good and evil, and upon eating from the tree (and thus sinning), they would gain that knowledge.

B. However, Adam and Eve were created as moral agents with the ability to discern between good and evil (e.g., obeying God = good; disobeying God = evil). The Serpent's temptation sheds more light on this subject.

C. The tempter basically argued that our first parents only thought they were free. True freedom, the Serpent quipped, is autonomous (a law unto oneself). Humankind, however, was created free but not autonomous. There are restrictions to our freedom, namely, that we are to be dependent upon our Creator, who is the only One who knows good and evil perfectly.

D. The Serpent challenged this notion by arguing that limited freedom is not freedom at all. He directly contradicted God's word by saying that Adam and Eve would not die when they ate of the tree. The only reason they were forbidden, according to the Serpent, was that God wanted to hold them back from reaching their fullest potential—doing what is right in one's own eyes.

E. Thus, the tree represented a knowledge that Adam and Eve were not meant to have until God's timing. And the heinous sin of the fall was the human grasp for autonomous freedom—taking from the tree regardless of God's word and independent of His guidance. This is what broke the covenant of creation.

F. Punishment for breaking the covenant was supposed to bring immediate death. Adam and Eve did suffer spiritual death that day, but God graciously stayed His hand from killing them physically. He instead killed an animal for its skin, so the two humans could be covered (this prefigured the Messiah's covering of His people with His righteousness). The biblical story from Genesis 3 onward is the story of God's work of redemption.

II. The Curse

A. The first thing to recognize about this curse is that it carried with it its antithesis: blessing.

B. Man: While Adam was already a tiller of the garden, the ground would now yield reluctantly.

C. Woman: The woman's pain in giving birth would now be greatly increased.

D. Serpent: The curse against the Serpent was that it would crawl on its belly. It also received the damning oracle that a Seed from the woman will crush the Serpent's head—not without damage to the Seed's heel. The irony here is that the very first proclamation of the gospel comes amid the curse of the fall.

E. God's first redemptive act occurred when Adam and Eve, ashamed of their nakedness, were covered with animal skins through the shedding of blood. This foreshadows the righteous garments of Christ that cover our nakedness—garments that also came through the shedding of blood.

STUDY QUESTIONS

1. Did Adam and Eve know what was evil before they ate of the forbidden tree?
   a. Yes
   b. No
   c. Maybe
   d. I don't know.

2. True freedom, according to the Serpent, _____ .
   a. Is impossible
   b. Is autonomous
   c. Is trusting in God's word
   d. None of the above

3. Adam and Eve were to be dependent on _____ for their knowledge of good and evil.
   a. Each other
   b. The Serpent
   c. Adam
   d. God

4. The breaking of the covenant involved _____ .
   a. Eating of the forbidden tree

    b. The grasp for autonomous freedom

    c. God's forcing Adam and Eve to disobey Him

    d. Both a and b

5. Even amid the curse of the fall, we can see _____ .

    a. God's fear of man

    b. A promised blessing

    c. Both a and b

    d. None of the above

6. God's first redemptive act occurred _____ .

    a. At the cross on Calvary

    b. When Noah was saved from the flood

    c. When Adam and Eve were covered with animal skins

    d. Before the foundation of the world

DISCUSSION GUIDE

1. In your own words, explain what the Tree of Knowledge of Good and Evil represented and how the Serpent twisted it to serve his argument.

2. After reading the biblical account of the fall (Gen. 3), how would you explain the nature of the sin committed by Adam and Eve (eating an apple can't be all that bad, can it?)? What do you think their motives were in sinning?

3. When we speak of the origin of sin, on whom can the blame be laid? How do we reconcile this and the fact that God is sovereign over all events?

4. Explain the various elements of the curse of the fall, as well as the blessings implied therein. How was the moral and spiritual character of Adam and Eve affected after their fall into sin?

5. Why are we also guilty of Adam's first sin? Use Scripture to support your answer.

6. Using Scripture, show that the doctrine of depravity is clearly taught by its authors. Include in your answer what the Scriptures teach regarding how the image of God in humanity was affected and the time when we who are in Adam actually become depraved (in the womb or as children?).

7. How does God's "first redemptive act" prefigure the work of Christ?

SUGGESTED READING FOR FURTHER STUDY

Robertson, O. Palmer. *The Christ of the Covenants*, pp. 93–107
Vos, Geerhardus. *Biblical Theology: Old and New Testaments*, pp. 41–44

6

THE NOAHIC
COVENANT

Every covenant that God made with people after the fall is incorporated under the general heading "the covenant of grace." For God to provide a way of salvation after the original covenant was violated gives testimony to the marvelous grace of His being. Furthermore, since the fall created a wall of enmity between God and humanity, we could not know God except by some voluntary condescension on His part, as the Westminster Confession of Faith notes (7.1). Thankfully, God has been pleased to make such condescension to humanity, to reach out to His fallen creatures, and throughout the history of redemption He has done so by covenants.

The first covenant that we encounter after the fall of Adam and Eve is called the Noahic covenant; that is, the covenant that God made with Noah. There are some very important dimensions to the Noahic covenant, but in order for us to grasp them, we have to try to fill in the blanks between the time of the fall of Adam and Eve and the appearance of Noah on the historical scene.

Immediately after the fall, there was a radical expansion of evil. This was manifested initially in the unspeakable horror of fratricide, when Cain, out of jealousy, murdered his brother Abel (Gen. 4). The Bible tells us that the ground was covered with the blood of Abel, and that blood, as it were, called out for vengeance before God (v. 10). So, we read of God's curse upon Cain (vv. 11–12). But there was a third son of Adam and Eve, whose name was Seth (v. 25). Following the murder of Abel by Cain, there is a brief genealogy of Cain (vv. 16–24). Likewise, following the account of the birth of Seth, there is an extended genealogy of his line (Gen. 5).

When we come to Genesis 6, we read: "Now it came to pass, when men began to multiply on the face of the earth, and daughters were born to them, that the sons of God saw the daughters of men, that they were beautiful; and they took wives for themselves of all whom they chose" (vv. 1–2). This is another foreboding introductory statement, because immediately after this apparently incidental report of the intermarriage of the sons of God and the daughters of men, we see the expansion of evil reach such a degree that we read:

> And the LORD said, "My Spirit shall not strive with
> man forever, for he is indeed flesh; yet his days

shall be one hundred and twenty years." There were giants on the earth in those days, and also afterward, when the sons of God came in to the daughters of men and they bore children to them. These were the mighty men who were of old, men of renown. Then the LORD saw that the wickedness of man was great in the earth, and that every intent of the thoughts of his heart was only evil continually. And the LORD was sorry that He had made man on the earth, and He was grieved in His heart. So the LORD said, "I will destroy man whom I have created from the face of the earth, both man and beast, creeping thing and birds of the air, for I am sorry that I have made them." But Noah found grace in the eyes of the LORD. (vv. 3–8)

What is going on here? First of all, what did God mean when He said, "My Spirit shall not strive with man forever"? The concept of striving here has to do with the Spirit exercising restraint. We have to understand that as much sin as there is in the world, as much sin as there is in our lives, we would all be much more wicked than we actually are were it not for the grace of the restraining power of God. In Reformed theology, we distinguish between total depravity and utter depravity. We say that fallen humanity is totally depraved, meaning that depravity penetrates the whole of our humanity—our minds, our wills, our hearts, and our bodies. But we are not utterly depraved, in which case we would be as bad as we possibly could be. The reason we are not as bad as we possibly could be is because God has placed restraints on us.

One of the interesting exercises I used with my seminary students was to ask them to list the people they regarded as the most wicked people who had ever lived. Inevitably, the names that came up were the emperor Nero, Adolf Hitler, Joseph Stalin, and other people of that ilk. These people all have something in common—they were dictators who had unlimited national power. There were no restraints upon them within their countries. The only restraints on Hitler or Stalin were put in place by other countries. But in their own spheres of authority, they were unrestrained. That's where we get the idea that power corrupts and that absolute power corrupts absolutely, as Lord Acton (1834–1902) famously said. I believe this adage is largely true (except when it is applied to God, who has absolute power but is totally uncorrupted by it). The idea is that if all restraints on the human heart are taken away, unspeakable evil begins to reign.

That is what God is threatening in Genesis. He was saying: "I've had enough of this. I'm going to remove the restraints." At that point, the desires of the human heart were only wicked continually. Therefore, God decided to destroy His creation with the flood.

TWO LINES OF DESCENT

But in the midst of this account, we have this incidental report of the intermarriage of the sons of God and the daughters of men.

Many people think this is a reference to a kind of celestial rape of human women by angels, because there are occasions in the Bible when angels are described as "the sons of God" (Job 1:6; 2:1). The idea is that angels came down, intermarried with women, and produced a bizarre race of radically evil people. I don't think that's what the Bible means at all. I think the clue to understanding what is going on here lies in the genealogies of Cain and Seth. We see these two lines coming down from Adam and Eve, but they are very different. If we look carefully, we can see that the line of Cain is the begetting of one criminal after another. Cain's line reads like a rogues' gallery, where the sin of the father, Cain, is revisited and recapitulated in the lives of his descendants. In stark contrast, when we look at the line of Seth, we see one godly person after another, culminating with Enoch, who "walked with God; and ... was not, for God took him" (presumably he was translated directly into heaven) (Gen. 5:24). So, these two lines are clearly distinguished, and those who are obedient to God can be called the "sons of God," while those who are disobedient can be called the "daughters of men." I think what we have here is the intermarriage of the descendants of Seth, who were obedient, and the descendants of Cain, who were wicked. The descendants of Seth took wives from the line of Cain, and these two lines became merged and blended. As a result, the sin that is so characteristic of the line of Cain engulfed the descendants of Seth, and the whole world was plunged into radical evil.

But we are told, and this is important for our understanding of this covenant, that "Noah found grace in the eyes of the LORD." It is the grace of God, then, that defined God's relationship with Noah. Furthermore, as we proceed through Genesis 6, we read: "This is the genealogy of Noah. Noah was a just man, perfect in his generations. Noah walked with God" (v. 9). We have to be careful here; this verse does not mean that Noah was without sin. The word *perfect* here means "complete." As people went in that world, Noah was in a class by himself. He stood out from the rest of ruined humanity. To say "Noah walked with God" was the highest compliment a human being could be given at that point in redemptive history.

Then we're told: "And Noah begot three sons: Shem, Ham, and Japheth. The earth also was corrupt before God, and the earth was filled with violence. So God looked upon the earth, and indeed it was corrupt; for all flesh had corrupted their way on the earth" (vv. 10–12). At this point, God announced to Noah that "the end of all flesh has come before Me, for the earth is filled with violence through them; and behold, I will destroy them with the earth" (v. 13). So, He gave Noah the instructions for building the ark and commanded him as to what to bring into the ark. Therefore, we read: "So Noah, with his sons, his wife, and his sons' wives, went into the ark because of the waters of the flood.... And the LORD shut him in" (Gen. 7:7, 16b). Then the waters of the flood came upon the earth, but Noah, his family, and all the animals in the ark were delivered.

GOD'S COVENANT WITH NOAH

After the floodwaters receded, Noah and his family emerged from the ark. It was then that God made His covenant with Noah:

"Then Noah built an altar to the LORD, and took of every clean animal and of every clean bird, and offered burned offerings on the altar. And the LORD smelled a soothing aroma. Then the LORD said in His heart, 'I will never again curse the ground for man's sake, although the imagination of man's heart is evil from his youth; nor will I again destroy every living thing as I have done. While the earth remains, seedtime and harvest, cold and heat, winter and summer, and day and night shall not cease'" (Gen. 8:20–22). Later we read: "Then God spoke to Noah and to his sons with him, saying: 'And as for Me, behold, I establish My covenant with you and with your descendants after you, and with every living creature that is with you: the birds, the cattle, and every beast of the earth with you, of all that go out of the ark, every beast of the earth. Thus I establish My covenant with you: Never again shall all flesh be cut off by the waters of the flood; never again shall there be a flood to destroy the earth'" (9:8–11).

So, the covenant that God made with Noah involved promises. God said: "I'm making a promise. I'm not going to destroy the earth with a curse again, and I'm not going to destroy every living thing as I have done. While the earth remains, the pattern, the rhythm, the cycle of nature will continue until the world is redeemed."

This is important because it reveals that the beneficiaries of God's covenant of grace, in addition to human beings, are the plant kingdoms, the animal kingdom, indeed, the whole earth. Remember, the whole earth was subjected to the curse because of the fall of the ones whom God had set as His vice-regents over the earth. He gave them dominion over the earth, the animals, the fish, the ground, and all things. When they fell, the curse that beset humanity also fell upon the earth. But Scripture tells us that with our redemption comes the redemption of the entire earth. We say that Jesus is "the cosmic Christ" because He brings cosmic redemption. Paul said, "We know that the whole creation groans and labors with birth pangs together until now" (Rom. 8:22). So, creation is awaiting its final redemption, but until then, God promises that He will not destroy it again.

We also read:

> So God blessed Noah and his sons, and said to them: "Be fruitful and multiply, and fill the earth. And the fear of you and the dread of you shall be on every beast of the earth, on every bird of the air, on all that move on the earth, and on all the fish of the sea. They are given into your hand. Every moving thing that lives shall be food for you. I have given you all things, even as the green herbs. But you shall not eat flesh with its life, that is, its blood. Surely for your lifeblood I will demand a reckoning; from the hand of every beast I will require it, and from the hand of man. From the hand of every man's brother I will require the life of man." (9:1–5)

Here we see that the Noahic covenant is, in many regards, a reconstitution of the covenant of creation. It is not a covenant that

God made with a certain ethnic group, such as Abraham and his descendants. Rather, Noah was functioning in a capacity similar to that of Adam before the fall. God had wiped out all of the wicked descendants of Adam and was beginning again, as it were. He was reordering and restructuring the covenant of creation. That's why this covenant includes some obligations that are very similar to the obligations God gave to Adam and Eve. He told them, "Be fruitful and multiply; fill the earth and subdue it; have dominion over the fish of the sea, over the birds of the air, and over every living thing that moves on the earth" (Gen. 1:28). Now that command is reiterated to Noah.

CAPITAL PUNISHMENT COMMANDED

God's mandate to Noah includes one of the most misunderstood and controversial texts from all of Genesis: "Whoever sheds man's blood, by man his blood shall be shed; for in the image of God He made man" (9:6). Many people read this verse as something of a prophecy: "Those who live by the sword shall die by the sword." That's not what it is. Rather, it is the covenantal institution of capital punishment.

It is very significant that this principle was not given to Abraham or to Moses, with whom God made restricted covenants. Since the Noahic covenant is the reconstitution of the creation covenant, this principle given to Noah affects all of humanity. Every person in every generation in every culture is under this principle of capital punishment. This is in the imperative, a command: a murderer must be put to death. God doesn't give the magistrate just the right to carry out capital punishment; He gives the magistrate the duty to carry out capital punishment when a life is taken. That's what causes so much controversy.

I remember reading an article by Larry King in which he complained about Christians constantly protesting against abortion laws in the United States. He said he would not take the Christian community's protest against abortion seriously until Christians mobilized against capital punishment. When he said that, he revealed that he didn't understand the biblical rationale, which is the same in both cases. What is behind the church's protest against abortion and behind the Christian community's historic support for capital punishment is the concept of the sanctity of life. People who oppose capital punishment do so by appealing to the same principle, the idea that every human life is sacred, but they then conclude that if a person chooses to murder another human being, we only add to the desacralization of life by executing the murderer. The belief is that everyone's life is sacred, even that of a murderer, and so we have to do something besides retaliate with revenge. However, the point of the original establishment of capital punishment is not deterrence or even vengeance. It is to maintain God's directive that every human life is sacred.

God's rationale for requiring the death of the murderer is that, in a very real sense, the person who raises his hand to slay a human being is making an assault not just against a fellow human but against God, because every human being bears God's image.

When someone kills a human being, he kills someone who is bearing the image of God. God is saying that to be made in His image is so sacred and so holy, if someone wantonly destroys an image-bearer of God, that person forfeits his right to life and is to be executed. So, God established the death penalty, the punishment for murder, not just in the Mosaic economy but in the Noahic economy, giving it universal application.

Finally, God said:

> "This is the sign of the covenant which I make between Me and you, and every living creature that is with you, for perpetual generations: I set My rainbow in the cloud, and it shall be for the sign of the covenant between Me and the earth. It shall be, when I bring a cloud over the earth, that the rainbow shall be seen in the cloud; and I will remember My covenant which is between Me and you and every living creature of all flesh; the waters shall never again become a flood to destroy all flesh. The rainbow shall be in the cloud, and I will look on it to remember the everlasting covenant between God and every living creature of all flesh that is on the earth." And God said to Noah, "This is the sign of the covenant which I have established between Me and all flesh that is on the earth." (Gen. 9:12–17)

Here is another sign that the promises of the Noahic covenant are not simply local promises or ethnic promises, but apply to the whole world perpetually. God said, "Every time it rains and you see the rainbow in the sky, that is My sign. It marks the sacred promise that I am swearing to you, a promise that I will keep unto all generations." God promises to preserve His creation, for it is the context for His plan of redemption.

CHAPTER 6

STUDY GUIDE

INTRODUCTION

In the evil generation preceding the time of the great flood, only Noah walked with God. He stood in stark contrast to those whose actions and thoughts were continually evil. Finally, God had had enough. The sins of the earth were full, and it was time to start again. Making a covenant with Noah and his family, God chose to graciously save them from the perilous deep. In so doing, God subdued once again the chaotic waters and put his chosen one, Noah, in charge as the steward of creation. In this chapter, Dr. R. C. Sproul explains the Noahic covenant and its relationship to the overarching covenantal theme in Scripture.

SCRIPTURE READING

Genesis 8:20–9:27

LEARNING OBJECTIVE

To be able to summarize the most important elements of the Noahic covenant and how they relate to Scripture as a whole.

QUOTATION

And God blessed Noah and his sons and said to them, "Be fruitful and multiply and fill the earth.... I give you everything.... Behold, I establish my covenant with you and your offspring after you, and with every living creature that is with you ... that never again shall all flesh be cut off by the waters of the flood, and never again shall there be a flood to destroy the earth." And God said, "This is the sign of the covenant that I make between me and you and every living creature that is with you, for all future generations: I have set my bow in the cloud, and it shall be a sign of the covenant between me and the earth."

—Genesis 9:1, 3, 9–13

OUTLINE

I. The Noahic Covenant

A. We have already looked at the distinction between the covenants of grace and works, and have seen that every covenant after the fall is to be looked at under the heading of the covenant of grace.

B. The first covenant we come to in the biblical story after the creation covenant is broken is the covenant God made with Noah.

C. The social background building up to this covenant is described in the Bible as a wicked time (Gen. 6:5). There was a radical expansion of evil in the world that began most notably with the murder of Abel (4:1–12). The lines of Seth and Cain were then intermingled.

D. At the time of Genesis 6, wickedness spread exponentially as the "sons of God" took ungodly wives. All of the world was filled with evil, "but Noah found favor in the eyes of the LORD" (v. 8).

E. In Genesis 6:3, God declared that His Spirit would not abide in humanity forever. That is, He would allow people to rebel until their sin had reached its fullness.

The 120 years is probably the span of time between this proclamation and the flood, at which time God judged the people for their utter wickedness.

F. We must see that it is God who graciously restrains us from being utterly depraved (distinct from totally depraved). Once God removes His restraining hand, the door is open to unspeakable sin.

G. In Genesis 6:8, we see that God's favor was upon Noah. "Grace" is the definitive word in God's relationship with Noah. In verse 9 we see that Noah was "blameless," which means "complete"—not "sinless." When someone is said to "walk with God" or is described as "obedient to God," the highest compliment has been paid to that person.

II. Life after the Flood (Gen. 8:20ff.):

A. God ratified His covenant with Noah through sacrifice. The terms involved making promises (on God's part).

B. We gain another glimpse of God's redemption at this point. The beneficiaries of the covenant of grace are not only God's people, but the entire cosmos (Gen. 8:22; 9:9–10). This is why Paul described Christ Jesus as the cosmic Christ, the One who brings *all* of creation into reconciliation to Him.

C. Notice that in many respects, the Noahic covenant recapitulates elements from the creation mandate ("Be fruitful and multiply.... I give you everything [plants and animals]" [Gen. 9:1, 3].

D. Is Genesis 9:6 a mere truism that violent people meet violent deaths? In all probability it is more than that. It is the covenantal institution of capital punishment. Because this covenant is global in scope, so, too, is this mandate to be carried out globally.

E. God's people sanction capital punishment for the very same reason they abhor abortion—the sanctity of life. This punishment was given to preserve human life. Wanton killing is an attack on the life-giver Himself. Thus, the person forfeits his life.

F. The sign of the Noahic covenant: the rainbow. The terms of this promise cover the whole earth. It is perpetual, and the promise to preserve creation shall be kept by God's own word—which creation, by the way, is the realm in which His redemptive plan is enacted.

STUDY QUESTIONS

1. Every covenant after the fall can probably be categorized under the _____.

    a. Covenant of works

    b. Covenant of grace

    c. The Noahic covenant

    d. None of the above

2. The time building up to Noah's flood was _____.

    a. Filled with righteousness

b. Marked by the world's passion for serving God

c. Wicked and continually evil

d. Partially corrupt and partially righteous

3. Without God's restraining grace we would be _____.

    a. Partially depraved

    b. Totally depraved

    c. Utterly depraved

    d. Perfect

4. Noah's "blamelessness" meant that he was _____.

    a. Worthy of God's covenant

    b. Sinless

    c. Unchallenged in his devotion to God and His commandments

    d. None of the above

5. The covenant of grace _____.

    a. Benefits only those whom the Father had given to the Son

    b. Benefits the entire world

    c. Should not be distinguished from the covenant of redemption

    d. Should not be distinguished from the covenant of works

6. The sign of the Noahic covenant was _____.

    a. Circumcision

b. A raven

c. A dove

d. A rainbow

DISCUSSION GUIDE

1. Read 1 Corinthians 10:9–12. Given that the Old Testament stories were written down for our instruction, what might we glean from the Noahic flood story that teaches us how to avoid evil? What does it teach about how God worked in the world during that time?

2. What do you think was the main purpose of this period of biblical history in its relation to God's overall plan of redemption? To get at this answer, describe the development of the human race before the flood, as well as God's restraining grace upon humanity (cf. Gen. 6:3). Why did God allow sin to march proudly through this age?

3. What state would the world be left in if God were to remove His grace completely? Use Scripture to support your answer.

4. Using Scripture, show that humanity is totally depraved as opposed to utterly depraved.

5. How was God's purpose in redemption furthered by saving Noah and his family? What child of Noah's would be the carrier of God's work of redemption?

6. Was the arrangement God made after the flood only with humanity? If not, what else was it made with? What was the sign of this covenant? How does this covenantal sign relate to that with which the covenant was made?

7. Describe the major elements of the Noahic covenant (cf. Gen. 8:20–9:17). Looking at Genesis 8:20; 15:9–10; 17:10–11; and Exodus 24:5–8, what common practice or element always accompanied the ratification of a covenant? Explain why.

SUGGESTED READING FOR FURTHER STUDY

Robertson, O. Palmer. *The Christ of the Covenants*, pp. 109–125
Vos, Geerhardus. *Biblical Theology: Old and New Testaments*, pp. 45–55

7

THE ABRAHAMIC COVENANT (PART 1)

If there's any one person in the Bible whose name is associated with the concept of covenant, it is Abraham. In fact, Abraham is such an important person in redemptive history that he has been called the "father of the faithful." The New Testament looks back to the promises that God made to Abraham, seeing their fulfillment in the birth and ministry of Jesus. I mentioned earlier that in the *Magnificat*, Mary's song of praise to God, she spoke under the influence of the Holy Spirit of how God was fulfilling His promises to Abraham through her and her unborn baby (Luke 1:54–55). When the Apostle Paul used an Old Testament illustration to

illuminate the gospel and to demonstrate the doctrine of justification by faith, his primary example was Abraham (Rom. 4). So, we
need to spend some time looking at the circumstances, the terms,
and the content of the covenant that God made with Abraham. We
must keep in mind, however, that this covenant too is an extension
of the broader covenant of grace.

In Genesis 12, we read this account: "Now the LORD had said
to Abram: 'Get out of your country, from your family and from
your father's house, to a land that I will show you. I will make you
a great nation; I will bless you and make your name great; and you
shall be a blessing. I will bless those who bless you, and I will curse
him who curses you; and in you all the families of the earth shall
be blessed" (vv. 1–3). Here we see the sovereign, supernatural grace
of God being bestowed on a man who was a pagan, who lived in a
pagan country and, presumably, in a pagan family.

People often ask me how the doctrine of election relates to
biblical redemption. I often say to them, "Notice that God did
not call Abraham because Abraham stood alone as being righteous
among the Mesopotamians. Neither did He call Hammurabi out
of paganism. Rather, God sovereignly chose Abraham and entered
into a covenant with him based upon the divine promise."

God told Abraham to leave his home country and go to a land
God would show him. Even though Abraham was already advanced
in years, in response to this revelation, this divine mandate, he
left everything that represented security in his life—his family, his
country, and all the rest—and he went out, not knowing where he
was going, simply because God promised to give him a country.

The book of Hebrews makes much of Abraham's fidelity and his response to the promise of God (Heb. 11:8–10). But notice that there was much more to the promise than land: "I will make you a great nation; I will bless you and make your name great; and you shall be a blessing. I will bless those who bless you, and I will curse him who curses you; and in you all the families of the earth shall be blessed."

Many years ago, a Lutheran church in Wisconsin produced an overview of the Bible called the Bethel Bible Series. Each study included some kind of graphic that illustrated the content of the particular biblical episode that was being treated. With respect to the covenant that God made with Abraham, this slogan appeared: "Blessed to be a blessing." That was a succinct way to communicate the important truth that when God made His promise to Abraham, the idea was not that Abraham alone would receive the benefits that God was promising him. Yes, Abraham would be singularly blessed; he would be given a great name, and so on. But the purpose of his blessing was that, through him, the whole world would be blessed.

Think about the pattern of the covenant promise here. In this instance, God made a covenant with an individual. But the blessings of that covenant were to go not only to this individual and not only to his family, but also to the whole world. As we will see, the promise to Abraham is passed down to his son Isaac, and from Isaac to his son Jacob, and from Jacob to Jacob's seed, which became the nation of Israel. So, it went from one person to one nation. But then what happened? It came back to one person who personifies and embodies the corporate solidarity of the whole nation—Jesus Christ. Then, from Christ, the blessing again goes to every tongue, tribe, and nation. But in God's plan of redemption, it starts with one individual.

ABRAHAM'S GREAT REWARD

The swearing of the Abrahamic covenant is found in Genesis 15. It begins with these words: "After these things the word of the LORD came to Abram in a vision, saying, 'Do not be afraid, Abram. I am your shield, your exceedingly great reward.' But Abram said, 'Lord GOD, what will You give me, seeing I go childless, and the heir of my house is Eliezer of Damascus?' Then Abram said, 'Look, You have given me no offspring; indeed one born in my house is my heir!' (vv. 1–3). God said, "I am your reward." But Abraham was puzzled and said: "But, God, what will You give me? What's this reward that I'm going to get?"

Abraham was probably one of the wealthiest men in the world, if not the wealthiest. What do you give to a man who has everything? Abraham wanted only one thing—a child of his own. His heir was Eliezer of Damascus, who was not his son. There seems to be some cynicism here. Abraham seems to be saying: "What can You give me that could possibly satisfy me in light of the fact that You have withheld from me the thing I have most wanted in my life? I have all of these flocks and herds, but there's no reward here, Lord, because I'm childless." This is a thinly veiled complaint that Abraham was uttering. The last thing he expected was that the reward would involve progeny, because he was convinced that it was way too late for that, that he was too old to father a son.

But God had wonderful news for Abraham: "And behold, the word of the LORD came to him, saying, 'This one shall not be your heir, but one who will come from your own body shall be your heir.' Then He brought him outside and said, 'Look now toward heaven, and count the stars if you are able to number them.' And He said to him, 'So shall your descendants be'" (vv. 4–5).

Have you ever been in a rural area on a clear night, away from the glare of the city lights? Under such circumstances, if you look at the night sky, you are able to see a vast number of stars in the sky. In fact, on a clear night, you can see the Milky Way, which looks like a cloud because of the billions of stars it contains. This view was even more magnificent in the rarified atmosphere of the Holy Land. This was what Abraham saw as he looked up at the sky that was ablaze with stars. God told him to count them, but they are uncountable. So, the message came through to Abraham: "You're not just going to have one child; your descendants are going to be as the stars of the sky."

We have to ask why God waited until Abraham was an old man and his wife was apparently barren before beginning to fulfill His covenant promise to make of Abraham a great nation. The whole point of God's dealings with Abraham was to manifest clearly that the benefits of the covenant rest in the power and the grace of God alone. God was not saying, "Well, Abraham, if you really work at it, I'm going to help you to become great, and I will be your cheerleader as you cooperate with the gifts that I give you so that you can become the head of a great nation." No. Abraham was incapable of receiving these covenant blessings apart from the supernatural intervention of God Himself.

What did Abraham say? Did he say: "Surely You're exaggerating, O Lord. This can't possibly be true"? No. Abraham responded in a way that became the normative response to the covenant promises of God for all people in all history. It is because of this response that the Apostle Paul cited Abraham as his primary example to show that the just live by faith. We read: "And he believed in the LORD, and He accounted it to him for righteousness" (v. 6).

This is critical for us. Paul told us later that Abraham was not redeemed because of any of the works he performed in his lifetime. He was saved by faith, the same way any of us is saved. Did he believe in Jesus? He did not even know about Jesus. He perhaps knew the vague hints about a Savior contained in the *protoevangelium* (Gen. 3:15). Nevertheless, the principle that is involved here is the same for us: faith in the promise. God made a promise of redemption. Abraham believed God. And, we are told, God accounted that belief to him as righteousness.

Abraham was a child of Adam. That means Abraham was a sinner. In fact, the biographical record of Abraham in the book of Genesis shows his warts and all. So, the ground of his salvation was not his own works or his own merit. Rather, there was a reckoning or an accounting of righteousness for one who, in fact, did not possess righteousness. This is an illustration of the central theme of redemption in the New Testament, the truth that redemption is by imputation. The only way we get into the kingdom of God is by God's counting us as righteous when we are not righteous. It's not that by faith that we do something so meritorious that we suddenly fulfill the covenant of works. It's not that we do what Adam failed to do. No, the ground for Abraham's salvation, though he didn't know it, was the righteousness of Christ, and that righteousness is also the ground for our salvation.

This rules out the popular but mistaken idea that people in the Old Testament were saved one way and people in the New Testament are saved another way. If we look carefully at Romans 3–5, we see clearly that the way of salvation is exactly the same in the Old Testament and the New Testament. Abraham was saved by faith, and the ground of his salvation was the merit of the One who was to come, which was then transferred to his account. So, he was saved by Christ just as much as we are.

This is what the Protestant Reformation was all about. The Roman Catholic Church was saying that God does not declare a person righteous until righteousness inheres within the person. Rome taught that we couldn't have that internal righteousness without grace, without faith, or without Christ. We need all of that, but all of those things that help us on that journey have to yield inherent righteousness before God will declare us righteous. The whole point of the gospel is that God declares us righteous in His sight *before* we are inherently righteous. That was certainly the case with Abraham, who was counted righteous.

THE OVEN AND THE TORCH

The Genesis account continues: "Then He said to him, 'I am the LORD, who brought you out of Ur of the Chaldeans, to give you this land to inherit it.' And he said, 'Lord GOD, how shall I know that I will inherit it?'" (vv. 7–8). We are told that Abraham believed God's promise, but he still was befuddled and overwhelmed by the big question: "How can I *know* for sure?" It seems as if Abraham had already lost faith. At best it seems he trusted God but was hanging by his fingernails. He wanted a little more than God's promise.

Every Christian wrestles with this desire for greater certainty at some point. Anyone can believe *in* God; even the demons do that. Believing God Himself is the harder task. Believing God involves living on the basis of the Word of God and trusting the promises of God, even when we cannot see the results in front of us. In Abraham's case, God was exceedingly gracious to grant further assurance.

That brings us to what I believe is one of the most important texts in all of sacred Scripture. If I were imprisoned in solitary confinement and could have only one book with me, I'd want the Bible. If I could have only one book of the Bible, I would want the book of Hebrews. But if I could have only one chapter of the Bible, it would be Genesis 15, and if I could have only one verse of the Bible, it would be Genesis 15:17, where we read, "And it came to pass, when the sun went down and it was dark, that behold, there appeared a smoking oven and a burning torch that passed between those pieces."

It often happens at Christian conferences that people buy the speakers' books and then ask those speakers to sign the books. Sometimes they ask a speaker to write down his or her "life verse." The first time someone asked me to do that, I said, "What's that?" because I had never heard of a life verse. The person explained that it is a verse a person picks out as especially important and applicable for his life. I didn't really have a life verse and I still don't, so when I sign a book and people ask for my life verse, I always write down Genesis 15:17. The people thank me and then go away, and but an hour later or the next day they'll come up to me with a puzzled look and say: "I read Genesis 15:17. Are you sure you didn't make a mistake?" When I assure them I did not make a mistake, they always want to know what Genesis 15:17 means, so I explain.

To understand what this verse is about, we have to go back to the strange directions that God gave Abraham when he asked, "How shall I know that I will inherit it?" We read: "So He said to him, 'Bring Me a three-year-old heifer, a three-year-old female goat, a three-year-old ram, a turtledove, and a young pigeon.' Then he brought all these to Him and cut them in two, down the middle, and placed each piece opposite the other; but he did not cut the birds in two" (vv. 9–10). In essence, God said: "If you want to know for sure that My promises are reliable, go and get these animals and bring them here. Then cut their carcasses lengthwise, and set the pieces as a pathway on the ground." It was as if Abraham were arranging a gauntlet, and someone would have to move between the pieces.

Then we read:

> Now when the sun was going down, a deep
> sleep fell upon Abram; and behold, horror and
> great darkness fell upon him. Then He said to
> Abram: "Know certainly that your descendants
> will be strangers in a land that is not theirs, and
> will serve them, and they will afflict them four
> hundred years. And also the nation whom they
> serve I will judge; afterward they shall come out
> with great possessions. Now as for you, you shall
> go to your fathers in peace; you shall be buried at
> a good old age. But in the fourth generation they
> shall return here, for the iniquity of the Amorites
> is not yet complete." (vv. 12–16)

Abraham fell into a trance and heard the voice of God, who
told him to "know certainly." However, what follows is both a
reiteration and an expansion of God's promise. Abraham learned
that his descendants would be enslaved in another land for four
hundred years, but afterward God would free them and bring
them back to Canaan. But Abraham himself would die in peace
after a long life.

Then we come to my favorite verse in Scripture, verse 17, where
we find the account of "a smoking oven and a burning torch" that
pass between the pieces. This event is profoundly significant, and
we will consider it in depth in the next chapter.

CHAPTER 7

STUDY GUIDE

INTRODUCTION

The covenant made with the patriarch Abraham continues to see its fulfillment to this day. With each sinner's passage into so great a salvation, father Abraham's nation grows. The true Israel—made up of Jews *and* Gentiles—is indeed more numerous than the stars in heaven and the sands upon the shore. In this chapter, Dr. R. C. Sproul begins to explain the most important features of the Abrahamic covenant and proves God's utter faithfulness to it.

SCRIPTURE READING

Genesis 15

LEARNING OBJECTIVE

To be able to articulate the background of the Abrahamic covenant.

QUOTATION

> *"Look toward heaven, and number the stars, if you are able to number them." Then [the Lord] said to him, "So shall your offspring be." And [Abram] believed the* LORD, *and he counted it to him as righteousness.... When the sun had gone down and it was dark, behold, a smoking fire pot and a flaming torch passed between these pieces. On that day the* LORD *made a covenant with Abram, saying, "To your offspring I give this land [the land of Canaan]."*

—Genesis 15:5–6, 17–18

OUTLINE

I. The Abrahamic Covenant

A. In redemptive history, the patriarch Abraham emerged as "the father of the faithful." Mary herself made mention of him: "He has helped his servant Israel, in remembrance of his mercy, as he spoke to our fathers, to Abraham and to his offspring forever" (Luke 1:54–55). Paul also used Abraham as the preeminent example of justification by faith (Rom. 4).

B. In Genesis 12:1–4, God called out a pagan among pagans, and Abraham responded in faith. Elements of the covenant include the following:

1. Abraham's offspring would be made into a great nation.

2. His name would be great.

3. People would be blessed or cursed depending on their relationship to him.

4. All the nations and families of the earth would be blessed through Abraham's blessing.

C. The pattern of the promise is as follows: the promise is given to one (Abraham), and blesses the many (ethnic Israel); it then comes back to One (the Christ), and then goes back to the many (the true Israel—Jews and Gentiles).

D. At the beginning of Genesis 15, we see Abraham ask the Lord about the heir who was promised to him. It stems from Abraham's faith in the promise, but the problem was that Abraham had grown old.

E. Why did God wait? Was Abraham under judgment? Maybe God wanted to clearly manifest that the benefits of His covenant relied completely on His grace. That is, it gave God the opportunity to glorify His holy name.

F. Genesis 15:6: "And [Abraham] believed the LORD, and he counted it to him as righteousness." This text was Paul's main proof from the Old Testament that justification was always by faith and not works. The Apostle contended that the just shall live by faith. In this way, Christ Jesus' righteousness was imputed to those before His death in the same manner as it is even unto to this very day.

G. Abraham, in faith, still wondered how he could be certain that he would inherit the land (v. 8).

H. Genesis 15:17 serves as the answer to Abraham's search for assurance: "When the sun had gone down and it was dark, behold, a smoking fire pot and a flaming torch passed between these pieces."

I. God Himself passed through the gauntlet alone, signifying that He alone is subject to the covenant curses if He does not follow through with the promises of the covenant. In our next chapter, we will explore more deeply this dramatic event in redemptive history.

STUDY QUESTIONS

1. The preeminent example of a faithful man in the letter to the Romans is _____.

a. Adam

b. Abel

c. Abraham

d. None of the above

2. Which patriarch emerged as the one most closely associated with redemptive history?

a. Jacob

b. Noah

c. David

d. None of the above

3. Which of the following is not an element of the Abrahamic covenant?

a. Abraham's name will be great.

b. Abraham's offspring will be made into a great nation.

c. All the nations of the earth will be cursed through him.

d. All of the above

4. Which of the following is an element of the Abrahamic covenant?

a. Nations will be blessed or cursed depending on their relationship to Abraham.

b. All the nations and families of the earth will be blessed through Abraham's blessing.

c. All of Abraham's offspring will be included in the kingdom of God.

d. Both a and b

5. In the letter to the Romans, Paul cited which text from the Old Testament as proof that justification is by faith alone?

    a. Genesis 15:2

    b. Genesis 15:17

    c. Genesis 15:6

    d. Genesis 16:3

6. Abraham's thirst for assurance came from his _____.

    a. Unbelief in God's promises

    b. Faith in God's promises

    c. Uncertainty in God's ability to give him a son

    d. None of the above

DISCUSSION GUIDE

1. Read Genesis 12:1–9. What promises did God make to Abraham?

2. After reading Genesis 15, describe in your own words the events therein. How did this advance God's work of redemption in the world?

3. Read Jeremiah 34:18–19. How does it relate to the ceremony described in Genesis 15? What does it say regarding the penalty that would fall upon the one who broke the covenant?

4. Why is Genesis 15:6 so significant for us today (i.e., those of us in the new covenant)?

5. Read Genesis 18:17–19. What was God's purpose in choosing Abraham? How does this serve to advance His work of redemption?

6. How did Abraham's faith relate to the promises of God (did Abraham actually see any of the promises actualized?)? Why did God tarry so long before fulfilling those promises? Did it benefit Abraham? What might it have taught him?

7. Is there any room in this narrative to suggest that Abraham may have believed in or served many gods? From Scripture, point out that Abraham's faith was monotheistic.

SUGGESTED READING FOR FURTHER STUDY

Robertson, O. Palmer. *The Christ of the Covenants*, pp. 127–46
Vos, Geerhardus. *Biblical Theology: Old and New Testaments*, pp. 66–81

8

THE ABRAHAMIC COVENANT (PART 2)

Genesis 15:17 is an exceedingly strange verse of Scripture for modern readers. We could read it a thousand times, but if we are not at least somewhat familiar with the customs of the Old Testament Semites, we will miss the significance of what is going on here.

I would venture to say that most Christians are basically familiar with the concept of a theophany. The word *theophany* is made up of two Greek words that are conjoined. The first, *Theo* or *Theos*, means "God." The root word is *phaneros*, which means "to make manifest." So, a theophany is a manifestation of God. We know that God is a spirit, having no body. We cannot perceive

Him with our normal vision because He is invisible, but there are times in biblical history when He makes Himself visible, as it were, by manifesting Himself through some means of the created order. For example, when God met Moses in the Midianite wilderness, He appeared as a bush that was burning but was not consumed. During the exodus, the people of God were led by a pillar of cloud by day and by a pillar of fire by night. These were theophanies.

Likewise, the "smoking oven" and "burning torch" in Genesis 15:17 are theophanies. They represent God. So, God is no longer merely speaking to Abraham; He is manifesting Himself.

What is most significant in this manifestation is what the oven and the torch did. In his vision, Abraham saw the theophany move between the pieces of animals laid out in two lines. In this drama, God was enacting something for Abraham, going through this action in order to give Abraham assurance and certainty of the reliability of His promise to him.

We know from extrabiblical sources that covenants in antiquity often were ratified by some kind of cutting rite. Later in the life of Abraham, we will see God instituting the sign of circumcision, the removal of the foreskin. But here in Genesis 15, there is cutting, too—the animals have been cut apart. By moving through these pieces, God was dramatizing His promise. By doing this, He was saying, "Abraham, if I fail to keep My promise to you, may I be ripped apart, may I be cut asunder, even as you have cut apart these animals." Notice that Abraham did not walk the gauntlet—only God did. The promise is all one-sided. God said, "I will bring these things to pass, Abraham, and I swear it by Myself."

In the New Testament, the author of Hebrews looked back to this moment in redemptive history and wrote, "For when God made a promise to Abraham, because He could swear by no one greater, He swore by Himself" (6:13). God could not say to Abraham: "If it will help you trust Me, I will raise My right hand and put My left hand on a Bible, and I'll swear an oath." There is nothing higher than God. There is nothing greater than God that He could call as a witness to His oath. He could swear only by Himself. And this is what He was doing when He made this covenant promise to Abraham and to his seed. He was saying, "Abraham, if I don't keep My covenant, if I don't keep My promise, may the immutable God have a mutation, may the eternal God fall into temporality, may the infinite become finite" (all of which is impossible). God was reinforcing His promise by swearing by His eternal, self-existent, and holy character.

Obviously, when God swears an oath, there is no possible higher level of certainty than that. So, when we struggle with our faith, wondering whether the promises of God are really trustworthy, it is good to come back to this verse. That's why I treasure this verse so highly. I say: "Lord, not only did You promise, You sealed that promise with this vow by Your own nature. You have sworn an oath by Yourself." That is truly comforting for me.

This is why the principle of covenant is so basic to the Christian life. It is because the covenant is based on promises.

This raises the question of whether the Abrahamic covenant is conditional or unconditional. Abraham had already exercised faith. That leads people to say: "The promises of God depend upon our having faith. We cannot receive any of the benefits of Christ and His covenant without faith." So, in one sense, the promises are conditional. But the Reformed faith has a distinct twist on this, for it teaches not just election but unconditional election, meaning that the electing grace that God gives to those whom He saves is not based on some condition that He sees in them, but it is sovereignly based in the good pleasure of His will. Even though He assigns the mediating necessity of faith, He acts to meet the condition for His people.

Here is what the Westminster Confession says in its chapter titled "Of God's Covenant with Man": "Man, by his fall, having made himself incapable of life by that covenant [the covenant of works], the Lord was pleased to make a second, commonly called the covenant of grace; wherein He freely offers unto sinners life and salvation by Jesus Christ; requiring of them faith in Him, that they may be saved, and promising to give unto all those that are ordained unto eternal life His Holy Spirit, to make them willing, and able to believe" (7.3).[1] So, God requires faith, but to everyone He Himself has ordained to eternal life He gives His Holy Spirit, who in turn makes them willing and able to have faith. God sets a condition and then makes it possible for certain ones to meet the condition.

THE CONTENT OF THE COVENANT

What is the content of the covenant that God made with Abraham? First, Abraham was going to possess the land of Canaan, which was not his by any birthright (Gen. 12:1, 7). Second, God promised that Abraham would be a great nation (v. 2a). For that to happen, Abraham had to have a huge number of descendants, which he had no reason to expect he could produce by any power within him or his wife. Third, Abraham would be a blessing to the world (v. 2b).

In time, these three promises are brought to pass on the basis of what we call monergism. When we talk about monergism, we're talking about a work that is performed by a single actor. In this case, that actor is God. The content of the promise that God made to Abraham was brought to pass not by a joint effort of God and Abraham. This was not a covenant of equals. Rather, the promises were brought to pass sovereignly and supernaturally by God.

For instance, God was the One who brought Abraham children. Again and again the Genesis account labors the point that both Abraham and his wife, Sarah, were too old to have children. When God gave this promise to Abraham, Abraham was already an old man, but then years went by and the promise remained unfulfilled. Eventually, as the last vestiges of hope that they would have a child of their own by natural means faded away with the years, Abraham and Sarah began to panic. Sarah came up with a solution: "Please, go in to my maid; perhaps I shall obtain children by her" (Gen. 16:2b). Sarah was saying: "Why don't you take my handmaiden, Hagar. I'm barren, but she's still fertile. If we're going to see this promise fulfilled, we have to cooperate with God. We have to do our part to make it come to pass."

So, Abraham went with Hagar, and Hagar produced a child whose name was Ishmael. But thirteen years later, when Abraham was ninety-nine years old, God came to him and renewed His promise that Abraham would have a son by Sarah. He said: "I will bless [Sarah] and also give you a son by her; then I will bless her, and she shall be a mother of nations; kings of peoples shall be from her" (Gen. 17:16). Essentially, God was saying: "Ishmael is not the child of promise. My covenant with you is that one from your own loins and from your wife is going to be your heir. Did you think you could work this out with your own schemes and plots? No." After all, God had made the promise to two people who were past the age of childbirth to make it absolutely clear that it was His doing.

I believe that the hardest thing for people to grasp in the Christian faith is that salvation is of the Lord. It is God who saves. The story of Abraham leaves no doubt about this. Abraham and Sarah's son, Isaac, was born completely through the power of God. God brought the descendants of Abraham into the Promised Land. The book of Joshua is replete with references that the conquest of Canaan is the Lord's work, not the work of the armies of Israel. It is supernatural, and so is God's redemption of His people.

As the story progresses, the covenant promise that was given to Abraham was then passed on to Isaac. It is significant that not every son of Abraham received the promise; Ishmael did not receive it because he was not the child of promise. Paul made this point in the New Testament. He wrote: "Nor are they all children because they are the seed of Abraham; but, 'In Isaac your seed shall be called'" (Rom. 9:7). This goes back to God's electing grace.

The same selection occurred in the next generation. Isaac's wife, Rebekah, bore him twins, Esau and Jacob. It was the custom in the ancient Near East that the familial blessing, also called the patriarchal blessing, went to the oldest son. He was the male heir of the family blessing. In the case of Isaac's two sons, Esau was the older twin. However, Jacob received the promise of the covenant. Why was the custom set aside? Once again, Paul answered: "When Rebecca also had conceived by one man, even by our father Isaac (for the children not yet being born, nor having done any good or evil, that the purpose of God according to election might stand, not of works but of Him who calls), it was said to her, 'The older shall serve the younger.' As it is written, 'Jacob I have loved, but Esau I have hated'" (Rom. 9:10–13). God made a judgment before the twins were born, neither having done any good or evil. Jacob received the blessing, but not because of anything he had done. It was by God's choice.

Many people believe that divine election is based on actions that God foresees. However, Paul could not have been clearer—God did not foresee some difference in behavior between Esau and Jacob. Furthermore, what was there in the life of Jacob that might cause God to choose Jacob rather than Esau? Jacob was a liar, a supplanter, and a cheater from the beginning. But God gave the covenant promise to him so that His sovereign grace in salvation should be made manifest.

Jacob, in turn, had twelve sons, but again, the oldest son did not receive the promise. This is why Paul could say "they are not all Israel who are of Israel" (Rom. 9:6). In other words, simply being of the line of Jacob, or Israel, is not enough. The promise is not given indiscriminately to Abraham's descendants. This was what Jesus made clear in His debate with the Pharisees: "They answered and said to Him, 'Abraham is our father.' Jesus said to them, 'If you were Abraham's children, you would do the works of Abraham'" (John 8:39). The Pharisees were true descendants of Abraham. They could show their biological inheritance all the way back to the patriarchs. But while they might have been natural children of Abraham, they were not children of the promise. God had not chosen them to receive the covenant promise of redemption that He had made to their father Abraham.

THE ROLE OF CIRCUMCISION

What of circumcision, the sign of the covenant? After Isaac was born, Abraham was circumcised, as a sign of this covenant promise, when he was an adult (Gen. 17:24). Isaac, his son, was given the sign of the covenant as an infant (21:4). That's very significant. Abraham was circumcised after he had faith while Isaac was circumcised before he had faith because the promise of God is given to all who believe, but not, simply, after they believe. The promise is the promise, whether it's received before one believes or after.

What was the significance of this sign? In the ancient Near East, circumcision was not restricted to Jews. It was administered widely as a cleansing rite, a sign of regeneration, purification, and sanctification for one born unclean. That's one of the points of parallel between baptism and circumcision. Both are signs of the covenant and both are signs of cleansing. But neither one of them automatically conveys what it signifies; rather, each shows the response of those who have received the benefits of the covenant, who are swearing fidelity and obedience to the God of all grace who redeems them. The rite is not on the grounds of their obedience. Our obedience is to be a response of gratitude to the One who saved us before we did any of the works of the law.

CHAPTER 8

STUDY GUIDE

INTRODUCTION

We have begun to see that God's covenant with humanity is gracious and everlasting, resting on His oath that should it fail, He will be torn in two (Gen. 15). The covenant, of course, by its very nature includes the response of the individual. "Abraham believed God, and it was reckoned to him as righteousness" (see Gen. 15:6). But never are the works of humanity the deciding factor in whether or not this covenant gets fulfilled. No, God was fully aware that fallen people could not obey perfectly, so He had (as we have already seen) an eternal plan to send One who would be perfect on their behalf. In this chapter, Dr. R. C. Sproul explores the various elements of the Abrahamic covenant.

SCRIPTURE READINGS

Genesis 17; 35:1–17

LEARNING OBJECTIVE

To be able to summarize the most important elements of the Abrahamic covenant and how they relate to Scripture as a whole.

QUOTATION

And God said to him, "Your name is Jacob; no longer shall your name be called Jacob, but Israel shall be your name." So he called his name Israel. And God said to him, "I am God Almighty: be fruitful and multiply. A nation and a company of nations shall come from you, and kings shall come from your own body. The land that I gave to Abraham and Isaac I will give to you, and I will give the land to your offspring after you."

—Genesis 35:10–12

OUTLINE

I. The Abrahamic Covenant (Continued)

A. In Genesis 15:8, Abraham asked God the suspenseful question, "How am I to know that I shall possess it [the land]?" God then answered by passing through the animal halves alone.

B. Just a rudimentary understanding of ancient Near Eastern customs will help us better understand what has taken place in Genesis 15:17. Often in the ancient Near East, covenants were ratified by the act of cutting (e.g., circumcision, as a sign of the covenant). By passing through the animal halves alone, God was saying that He would experience the curse of the covenant by being ripped in two if He failed to keep it.

C. The symbols used to describe God as He passed through the gauntlet were a smoking pot and a flaming torch, both reminiscent of the exodus and the pillars of smoke and fire that led the Israelites (the primary audience of the book of Genesis) through the wilderness. This passing through the animal halves alone gave Abraham the assurance that the covenant would be fully and faithfully kept to the end.

D. The author of the epistle to the Hebrews hearkened back to this often:

1. It is impossible for God to die.

2. It is impossible for God to lie.

3. God could thus not swear by anything greater than His own name (which He did by passing through the gauntlet alone). Therefore, God's failing the covenant is manifestly impossible.

E. When Christians struggle with this assurance, we must ultimately look to the promises of God through Christ. When Abraham struggled, he had to look on the promises made by God in Genesis 15.

F. To be sure, Abraham's participation and obedience were integral to the covenant (cf. 15:6), but in order for the covenant to be everlasting, there must be a covenant keeper who is Himself eternally faithful.

G. In like manner, we are saved by the unconditional election of God. That is, God through Christ met the conditions of the covenant on our behalf. Faith grabs hold of this promise. Faith is trust in the finished work of Christ. It is not the same as a work of pious obedience, for faith is "the gift of God, not a result of works, so that no one may boast" (Eph. 2:8–9).

H. The Westminster Confession of Faith, 7.3, sums up this doctrine well. God requires faith in the finished work of Jesus Christ from those who may be saved. It is indeed the condition of the covenant. But that condition rests upon the condition that Jesus already met—that of perfect obedience. God graciously supplies the individual with the ability to meet the condition of faith, or trust, in the redemptive work of Christ on the individual's behalf.

I. This very same pattern is evident in the Abrahamic covenant.

II. The Content of the Abrahamic Covenant

    A. From Abraham a great nation will come (many in number).

    B. His progeny will own the land of Canaan (drinking from wells they did not dig, etc.).

    C. Abraham's offspring will be a blessing to all the nations of the world.

    D. All of these promises are ultimately brought to pass by the work of *one person*. The rest of Scripture records this story down to that one person.

    E. Abraham had a son, Isaac, and the covenant was then passed on to him (Gen. 26). The promise, however, was not given to all of Abraham's children (i.e., Ishmael). Nor was it always passed on to the eldest son. In Isaac's case, Jacob received the covenant instead of Esau.

    F. Paul belabored this point in Romans 9. For example, God, of His own free will, and not based on anything Jacob or Esau would or would not do, chose Jacob according to His eternal purpose (9:12–13).

    G. The covenant then passed down through Jacob to his twelve sons. Moses used this to charge the nation of Israel to recognize as their inheritance the land of Canaan, as well as motivate them to faithfully keep the covenant.

III. Circumcision: The Sign of the Covenant

A. God called on Abraham to be circumcised as a sign of the covenant between God and Abraham and his progeny (Gen. 17). While Abraham was circumcised after faith in God, Isaac was circumcised before he exhibited faith in God (21:4). Why was this done? Because the promises of God are given to all who believe, but not simply *after* they believe. The promise is a promise whether it is received before or after it is believed.

B. What did circumcision signify? As in other ancient Near East cultures, circumcision was a cleansing ritual. It was understood that infants come into the world unclean. Thus circumcision served as a sign of cleansing, regeneration, purification, and sanctification. But the sign itself (circumcision) and the thing signified (regeneration) are not one and the same.

C. Many Israelites, however, mistook their mere sign of being inside the covenant community as proof of their salvation. In like manner, the sacrament of baptism in the new covenant has been misunderstood in this way. The sign is one of God's fidelity to His promise to all who believe.

D. This is why we say that sanctification (good works) necessarily flows out of justification. It is not the grounds of our justification. Obedience (sanctification) is to be a response of gratitude to the One who saved us *before* we do any good works (or works of the law).

STUDY QUESTIONS

1. By passing through the animal halves alone, _____.

    a. God was saying that Abraham would experience the curse of the covenant by being ripped in two if he failed to keep it

    b. God was saying that He would experience the curse of the covenant by being ripped in two if He failed to keep it

    c. God was saying that Isaac would experience the curse of the covenant by being ripped in two if he failed to keep it

    d. None of the above

2. By which of the following was God represented when He passed through the gauntlet?

    a. A smoking calf

    b. A smoking pot

    c. A burning torch

    d. Both b and c

3. Since God cannot die or lie, and since He swore by His own name when He passed through the animal halves, then _____.

    a. Keeping the covenant is manifestly impossible

b. Failing the covenant is manifestly impossible

c. Failing the covenant is manifestly possible

d. None of the above

4. Was Abraham's participation and obedience integral to the covenant?

a. No

b. Yes

c. Sometimes

d. None of the above

5. Just like the Abrahamic covenant, election unto salvation is

_____.

a. Conditional

b. Dependent on a person's work

c. Unconditional

d. None of the above

6. What did circumcision signify?

a. Purification

b. Cleansing

c. Regeneration

d. All of the above

DISCUSSION GUIDE

1. How does the ceremony described in Genesis 15 (and in Jer. 34) relate to other ancient Near East cultures?

2. What purpose might God have had in setting aside ancient Near East customs as this covenant was passed down?

3. Does the covenant of grace ultimately rely on human obedience or God's faithfulness? Support your answer with Scripture.

4. How is the principle of God's sovereign election confirmed in the story of the patriarch? How did Paul use this story in his letter to the Romans? In what sense did the Apostle speak of election as universal (cf. Gal. 4:22ff.)? In what sense is it individual (cf. Rom. 9:6ff.)?

5. Show from Scripture what it is that circumcision signifies. Show that it is *not* a sacrificial ritual of bodily mutilation (i.e., show that Scripture would prohibit such a thing).

6. Explain how the teachings of Paul (and the rest of the New Testament) correct the view that one is saved simply by being given the sign of the covenant.

7. Read Leviticus 26:41; Deuteronomy 10:16; and 30:6. What spiritual meaning clearly enjoins itself to the act of circumcision

according to these texts? How does this pose a problem for those who would say that the old covenant was purely external in its aim (i.e., that it was not concerned with people's heartfelt responses to God)?

SUGGESTED READING FOR FURTHER STUDY

Robertson, O. Palmer. *The Christ of the Covenants*, pp. 147–66
Vos, Geerhardus. *Biblical Theology: Old and New Testaments*, pp. 81–99

NOTE

1. "Of God's Covenant with Man," *The Westminster Confession of Faith*, Center for Reformed Theology and Apologetics, accessed February 23, 2013, http://www.reformed.org/documents/wcf_with_proofs/.

9

THE MOSAIC
COVENANT
(PART 1)

The Mosaic covenant is certainly the most complicated of all of the biblical covenants, and the one that perhaps provokes the most controversy and confusion because of the complications of its content. Because the Ten Commandments are such an integral part of the Mosaic covenant, many Christians have seen this covenant as a way of salvation that God established in the Old Testament, by which people were rewarded with eternal life if they obeyed the Old Testament law. Some would say that this way of salvation is, in a sense, a reversion back to the covenant of works.

However, orthodox Christianity has generally recognized that there is only one way of salvation throughout all of history. In Romans 3–4, Paul labored the point that salvation occurred in the Old Testament in the same manner it occurred in the New Testament: by faith. Ultimately, the grounds for salvation at any time in redemptive history is the work of Christ. If that is true, then we should see the Mosaic covenant as an extension of the covenant of grace, or, if you will, as an extension of the Abrahamic covenant, which was made long before Moses lived.

Of course, there are difficult and confusing passages, such as John 1:17: "For the law was given through Moses, but grace and truth came through Jesus Christ." Likewise, Paul often contrasted the Old Testament law and the New Testament gospel, and that raised a whole list of questions with respect to the actual significance, purpose, and function of the law in the Old Testament, as well as its application to Christians in the New Testament. The question of the relationship between law and gospel remains one that divides Christians at significant points.

As we begin our attempt to understand the Mosaic covenant, I think it is worthwhile to point out that there are certain individuals who leap from the pages of the Old Testament and attain great importance. I would say that these three people in Old Testament history enjoy the most lofty status: Abraham, who is known as the father of the faithful; Moses, because of the significant role he played in the exodus and in the formation of the nation of Israel; and David, who became the model king for the future messianic kingdom that will be inaugurated by Jesus. So, Moses is one of those titans of the Old Testament.

AN EXTRAORDINARY BIRTH

The Bible gives much attention to the extraordinary circumstances of Moses' birth. Pharaoh ordered that the Hebrews' male children be slaughtered, so Moses' mother consigned him to the Nile River in a basket of woven reeds. He was found by the daughter of Pharaoh and reared in Pharaoh's household. Moses was then educated in all the arts and sciences of the Egyptians, only to be forced into exile after he attacked and killed an Egyptian who was mistreating one of Moses' kinsmen. So, he fled to the Midianite wilderness, where he spent several decades in exile until he reached old age (Exod. 2).

Then, of course, he had the extraordinary experience of the encounter with God at the burning bush, when God spoke to Moses audibly and revealed to him the divine name, the *tetragrammaton*, the sacred name of God, "I AM WHO I AM." Moses received the commission to return to Egypt and to declare to Pharaoh that God wanted His people, the Hebrews, to be released from their captivity so that they could go out into the desert and worship Him. Also, he was commissioned to go and tell the Hebrews, who were the slaves of Pharaoh, to leave Egypt under Moses' direction (Exod. 3). So, Moses became the key figure in the most important redemptive activity of the entire Old Testament, the exodus. This event, the exodus, is the historical context in which the Mosaic covenant was made.

I remind you, as I noted earlier, that God's revelation of His plan of redemption unfolds through history. We call that unfolding "progressive revelation." It does not correct what went before it, but expands the content and the information that God reveals in terms of His relationship to His chosen people. The Mosaic covenant represents another unfolding of God's revelation.

It is important for us to understand the roles Moses plays in the Old Testament, which, in many ways, anticipate the ministry of Jesus Himself. Moses is called the prophet of God to Israel. Through Moses, God revealed His Word. Likewise, Christ, also, is a prophet. Before Aaron was consecrated as the high priest of Israel, Moses was assigned the task of doing priestly work, so he participated in priestly directives, even as Christ is our Great High Priest. Moses never rose to the position of king because, during his life, Israel was not organized as a kingdom. In that regard, he did not anticipate Christ. However, Moses was the key leader of the nation and the deliverer of Israel, even as Christ is our Deliverer under the new covenant. So, in at least some respects, Moses anticipated Jesus' roles as Prophet, Priest, and King.

But most significant was the role of Moses as mediator. He was the mediator of the old covenant, the mediator between God and humanity, whereas Jesus is the Mediator of the new covenant. That's a significant role, one that should not be taken lightly in the history of God's people. As the mediator, Moses received the new revelation from God that was found in the law and communicated it to the people. Furthermore, Moses represented the people before God, interceding for them when they sinned.

REALIZATION OF THE PROMISES

During Moses' ministry, we see the promises that God had made to Abraham in the Abrahamic covenant finally coming to fulfillment. As we noted earlier, God promised that Abraham would be the father of a great nation, and that his descendants would multiply into a vast people. Also, God promised that Abraham's people would possess the Promised Land. Remember, Abraham never possessed the land except for a small plot where he was buried (Acts 7:5; Heb. 11:8; Gen. 23:20). Finally, God promised that Abraham would be a blessing to all nations.

When we read of Moses' ministry of mediation, we see that the descendants of Abraham, the people of Israel, are brought out of Egypt and organized as a nation. Here we see God sanctifying this group of slaves and gathering them to Himself, adopting them, as it were, as His sons and daughters, and establishing them in a theocratic political structure, with God as their King. So, the Hebrews became His chosen people, organized as a distinct nation.

Also under Moses' leadership, the people left Egypt, moved through the wilderness, and advanced to the border of the Promised Land. Moses himself did not enter the Promised Land, but it is due to his tutelage that the Israelites conquered the land under the leadership of his chief lieutenant, Joshua. So, we see the actualization in history of the Israelites gaining the land of Canaan, just as God had promised.

Finally, there is a realization of the promise that Abraham, through his descendants, would be a blessing to the nations. This is one of the consequences of the giving of the law through Moses. It has been said that the roots of contemporary civilization, particularly the law structures of the West, go back to the common law of England, which, in turn, reaches back to the jurisprudence of Rome and the legal structures of Greece. But preceding and influencing even those is the law of God in the Old Testament. Today, we see an ongoing struggle in the United States over the continuing utility of the Ten Commandments within our communities and our courts. But no matter how much resistance there may be today to any allusion to Old Testament law, no one can deny the historical reality that all of the world has been blessed through the influence of the Decalogue on the Western world. It had a formative influence on our own legal structures. That's why there's great irony in the attempts to repudiate it.

Also, the patriarchs' experience with God was enhanced during Moses' tenure. For example, when God visited Abraham, Isaac, and Jacob, He rarely appeared to them. We have the tendency to think back that God was appearing to Abraham every night, every time he had a dream. In truth, it was very rare for people to actually experience the presence of God in the patriarchal period.

During the life of Jacob, when he set out to flee from his brother Esau, he found a place to camp for the night, and he had a dream in which he saw a ladder reaching up to heaven, with the angels of God ascending and descending on it, and God standing at the top. When he woke, he said: "Surely the LORD is in this place, and I did not know it…. How awesome is this place!" (Gen. 28:16–17). This brief midnight manifestation of God to Jacob was an extremely critical moment in his life and his development. The patriarchs had such brief encounters with the presence of God periodically, but there was no sustained, consistent, continual manifestation of the presence of God in the midst of the people.

By contrast, during the ministry of Moses, God manifested Himself nearly constantly. He led the people in the theophanies of the pillar of cloud and the pillar of fire. When the religious structure of the new nation was inaugurated by divine instruction under Moses' leadership, the tabernacle was established according to the specific prescriptions of God, down to the last detail. The tabernacle represented the presence of God in the midst of the people. God was constantly present and accessible to the people. So, this idea of divine presence is very important in the unfolding of this covenant that God mediated through Moses.

Turning to the content of the Mosaic covenant, we find that there are various elements. I am forced to simplify my outline of these elements. As I noted above, the Mosaic covenant is very detailed and complex, and in the final analysis, it cannot really be reduced to a handful of elements. I simply want to try to hit the highlights of the content of this covenant that God made with Moses. I want to note, first, the exodus itself; second, the actual making of a covenant; third, the Decalogue, or the Ten Commandments; and fourth, the ritual or the ceremonial law. We will consider these elements in the next chapter.

CHAPTER 9

STUDY GUIDE

INTRODUCTION

By far the most complicated covenant to understand in its relation to the covenant of grace is the Mosaic covenant. This covenant was ratified at Mount Sinai and stands as the definitive marker of the age before Christ Jesus' work on earth. Much confusion abounds about the place of this covenant in redemptive history. In this chapter, Dr. R. C. Sproul seeks to explain the relationship of the law to the believer (both of the old covenant and new covenant), and discuss the mediating role of Moses in the old covenant.

SCRIPTURE READING

Deuteronomy 5–6

LEARNING OBJECTIVES

1. To understand how Moses served as the old covenant mediator.
2. To be able to list four elements of the Mosaic covenant.

QUOTATION

When I went up the mountain to receive the tablets of stone, the tablets of the covenant that the LORD made with you … written with the finger of God … on them were all the words that the LORD had spoken with you on the mountain out of the midst of the fire on the day of the assembly.

—Deuteronomy 9:9–10

OUTLINE

I. The Mosaic Covenant

    A. This is the simplest, most basic question we must ask when faced with this covenant in Scripture: "Is this covenant a reversion to the covenant of works we saw in the garden between prefall humanity and God?"

B. Romans 3 and 4 tells us that the law was not meant to be disjoined from the covenant of grace, for the Mosaic law could never save anyone. The works of the law are established by the believer who lives in faith (3:27–31).

C. The Mosaic covenant, then, must be seen as an extension of the covenant of grace. Still, how are we to understand the Apostolic contrast between Moses and Jesus, law and gospel?

II. Moses the Man

A. Three men in the Old Testament become virtual embodiments of the covenant. They are Abraham, Moses, and David.

B. Moses' place in redemptive history developed over time until he became the key figure in the past age as *the* mediator in God's plan of redemption. The exodus event from Egypt also became the key event that symbolized God's utter faithfulness to His covenant.

C. Two points in passing are that the revelation of the covenants in Scripture are to be seen as *progressive*. This does not mean that the previous revelation is superseded; it simply means that a subsequent revelation comes alongside the previous one and makes it more clear, or reveals more fully God's acts.

D. Another point is that while Jesus is under the new covenant, Moses was under the old. He was the prophet (the revealer of God's Word).

E. Moses as mediator: He communicated God's word to the people, and God's word to Abraham was actualized under Moses' leadership.

F. Under Moses' mediation

1. The people were gathered together and organized as a nation with their own laws and political structure.

2. The people were brought safely to the borders of the Promised Land.

3. All the people of the world have been blessed as a result of the writing of God's law.

4. God sustained His presence in the midst of Israel more than in previous times. From the burning bush to the glory cloud over the tabernacle, God made His presence known.

III. Four Elements of the Mosaic Covenant (These are not the only elements, but they are essential to understanding this covenant.)

A. The exodus: Note that the nation's redemption came *before* they were given the law. This pictures what is always true of God's salvation—it comes by free grace and sovereign choice. The people did not gain God's deliverance by obeying the law; rather, they watched as God acted on their behalf. This event became the pivotal event in Israel's history. In many ways the exodus anticipates the redemption found in Christ Jesus. The Christian partakes in an exodus from sin and death into life everlasting.

B. The making of the Mosaic covenant

C. The giving of the law

D. The ritual of the law

STUDY QUESTIONS

1. The Mosaic covenant _____.

      a. Falls under the auspices of the covenant of works

      b. Falls under the auspices of the covenant of grace

      c. Falls under the auspices of the Davidic covenant

      d. None of the above

2. Before the final sacrifice of Jesus Christ, one followed the Mosaic law _____.

      a. In order to be saved

      b. In gratitude for God's salvation

      c. To appease the anger of God

      d. None of the above

3. Seeing biblical covenants as "progressive" means that _____.

      a. The previous covenant is superseded

      b. All covenants before and after are separated and unrelated

      c. That a subsequent covenant comes alongside the previous one and reveals more fully God's acts

      d. None of the above

4. Under Moses' mediation _____.

    a. The Israelites were formed as a nation and entered the Promised Land

    b. All the people of the world are blessed by the writing down of God's law

    c. God sustained His presence among the Israelites

    d. All of the above

5. Just as in the exodus event, God's salvation _____.

    a. Comes before the law and by free grace and sovereign choice

    b. Comes after the law and by free grace and sovereign choice

    c. Comes before the law and by free grace and sovereign foreknowledge of those whom God saw would believe and keep faithful

    d. None of the above

6. Which of the following is not an element of the Mosaic covenant?

    a. The exodus

    b. The making of the covenant and the giving of the law

    c. Salvation by works

    d. The ritual of the law

DISCUSSION GUIDE

1. In your own words, explain why Moses became such a pre-eminent figure in the history of Israel.

2. Now using Scripture, show how Moses was instrumental in ushering in the great patriarchal promises (at least in their external embodiments).

3. Read Deuteronomy 18:18 and Hosea 12:13. Was Moses merely in a long line of prophets, or was he seen as their head?

4. Read Isaiah 10:26; 11:11; 63:11–12; Jeremiah 23:5–8; and Micah 7:15. Describe the ways in which Moses' work was connected to the great "latter days" when God would reestablish the Israelite kingdom.

5. Read Numbers 12:7 and Hebrews 3:1–6. Can Moses rightly be called the mediator of the old covenant? Why or why not?

6. How did Moses prefigure Christ with respect to his prophetic role (cf. Deut. 18:15)?

7. How did Moses prefigure the Messiah in his priestly role (cf. Exod. 14:31; 19:9; 24:4–8; 32:30–33)?

SUGGESTED READING FOR FURTHER STUDY

Robertson, O. Palmer. *The Christ of the Covenants,* pp. 167–85
Vos, Geerhardus. *Biblical Theology: Old and New Testaments,* pp. 100–120

10

THE MOSAIC COVENANT (PART 2)

In the previous chapter, I gave a short introduction to the Mosaic covenant. In this chapter, I want to touch on four elements of the covenant: first, the exodus itself; second, the actual making of a covenant; third, the Decalogue, or the Ten Commandments; and fourth, the ritual or the ceremonial law. These four elements are very important for the historical unfolding of the content of God's revelation to His people. Therefore, they should be important to us.

THE EXODUS FROM EGYPT

I think it is significant that these elements of the Mosaic covenant are revealed in this order according to the unfolding of the will of God, especially that the exodus occurs first. It is not that God first gave the law and then, on the basis of the people's obedience to the law, He redeemed them. Their redemption, their deliverance from bondage, came *before* the Decalogue was given. Israel's redemption in the exodus was a result of God's sovereign power and electing grace. He did not redeem His people because of their goodness, their merit, or their obedience. Rather, their salvation was of the Lord. He made clear in His victory over Pharaoh that He was the most powerful ruler on the face of the earth, and He defeated Pharaoh not by the might and the strength of the Israelites, who were fleeing from Egypt, but by miraculously opening the Red Sea and allowing His people to pass through while their enemies were engulfed by the returning waters.

So, the exodus is the critical juncture for redemption in the Old Testament. In a real way, it anticipates the coming of Christ, because Israel's redemption from the Egyptians is a salvation from slavery, from bondage. Of course, it is external bondage, but it prefigures the ultimate exodus of the people of God, an exodus from their bondage to sin and to the wiles of Satan. It is not just a geopolitical event, but a spiritual event. Of course, the exodus has strong overtones of spiritual redemption because God brought the people of Israel out to worship Him, that they might be holy, that He might be their God and they His people.

All the other elements of the old covenant are then added to the historical exodus. God did not just release some slaves from captivity and set them free to do whatever they desired. No, He brought them into freedom so that He could nurture them and bring them to Himself as His covenant people, that they might inherit the land of Canaan and be a blessing to the whole world.

THE MAKING OF THE COVENANT

There's something different about the way in which the Mosaic covenant is structured. I have emphasized that the earlier covenants were one-sided. For instance, God made the promise to give the blessings to Abraham, to make him a great nation, to give his family the land, and so on. But when we come to the Mosaic covenant, for the first time in the unfolding of the covenant relationships, we see the response of the people who swore an oath of loyalty to their covenant God. Still, even though the people were involved in this covenant, that does not mean they were equal partners. Again, God made the promises, then required the people to swear allegiance to Him.

It is interesting that this aspect of the covenant is set forth before the giving of the Decalogue. Most Christians are aware that the giving of the Ten Commandments is recorded in Exodus 20, but the actual giving of the covenant is found in Exodus 19. That chapter begins with these words:

> In the third month after the children of Israel had
> gone out of the land of Egypt, on the same day,

they came to the Wilderness of Sinai. For they had departed from Rephidim, had come to the Wilderness of Sinai, and camped in the wilderness. So Israel camped there before the mountain.

And Moses went up to God, and the LORD called to him from the mountain, saying, "Thus you shall say to the house of Jacob, and tell the children of Israel: 'You have seen what I did to the Egyptians, and how I bore you on eagles' wings and brought you to Myself. Now therefore, if you will indeed obey My voice and keep My covenant, then you shall be a special treasure to Me above all people; for all the earth is Mine. And you shall be to Me a kingdom of priests and a holy nation.' These are the words which you shall speak to the children of Israel."

So Moses came and called for the elders of the people, and laid before them all these words which the LORD commanded him. Then all the people answered together and said, "All that the LORD has spoken we will do." So Moses brought back the words of the people to the LORD. (vv. 1–8)

God began by calling attention to what He had done by way of redeeming the people. Then He called them to obey Him and keep His covenant, giving them magnificent promises—they shall be His treasure, and "a kingdom of priests and a holy nation." Thereafter, the people pronounced their promise of loyalty to the God of the covenant.

The narrative continues:

> And the LORD said to Moses, "Behold, I come to you in the thick cloud, that the people may hear when I speak with you, and believe you forever."
>
> So Moses told the words of the people to the LORD.
>
> Then the LORD said to Moses, "Go to the people and consecrate them today and tomorrow, and let them wash their clothes. And let them be ready for the third day. For on the third day the LORD will come down upon Mount Sinai in the sight of all the people. You shall set bounds for the people all around, saying, 'Take heed to yourselves that you do not go up to the mountain or touch its base. Whoever touches the mountain shall surely be put to death. Not a hand shall touch him, but he shall surely be stoned or shot with an arrow; whether man or beast, he shall not live.' When the trumpet sounds long, they shall come near the mountain."
>
> So Moses went down from the mountain to the people and sanctified the people, and they washed their clothes. (vv. 9–14)

In these verses, we see God spelling out the stipulations for the giving of the Ten Commandments. First, the people have to go through some form of purification. What we have in these rites of purification is the drama of expiation. When God brings a people into covenant relationship with Himself, He adopts them as His children, but He also sanctifies them; that is, He makes them holy or sets them apart. He does this through expiation, which is what is later called the remission of sins. It is the removal of wickedness from the people and from the camp. Because of their sin, they are not allowed to ascend the holy mountain, and even to receive the grace of the covenant they have to go through demonstrations of cleansing and sanctification.

Next, we read:

> Then it came to pass on the third day, in the morning, that there were thunderings and lightnings, and a thick cloud on the mountain; and the sound of the trumpet was very loud, so that all the people who were in the camp trembled. And Moses brought the people out of the camp to meet with God, and they stood at the foot of the mountain. Now Mount Sinai was completely in smoke, because the LORD descended upon it in fire. Its smoke ascended like the smoke of a furnace, and the whole mountain quaked greatly. (vv. 16–18)

This is a spectacular scene: thunder, lightning, thick clouds, the sound of a trumpet, fire, earthquake. The people were right to tremble. Interestingly, we see again the imagery of fire, such as we saw in Genesis 15, when God entered His covenant with Abraham by means of a theophany of a smoking oven and a burning torch.

The narrative then recounts:

> And when the blast of the trumpet sounded long and became louder and louder, Moses spoke, and God answered him by voice. Then the LORD came down upon Mount Sinai, on the top of the mountain. And the LORD called Moses to the top of the mountain, and Moses went up.
>
> And the LORD said to Moses, "Go down and warn the people, lest they break through to gaze at the LORD, and many of them perish. Also let the priests who come near the LORD consecrate themselves, lest the LORD break out against them."
>
> But Moses said to the LORD, "The people cannot come up to Mount Sinai; for You warned us, saying, 'Set bounds around the mountain and consecrate it.'"
>
> Then the LORD said to him, "Away! Get down and then come up, you and Aaron with you. But do not let the priests and the people break through to come up to the LORD, lest He break out against them." So Moses went down to the people and spoke to them. (vv. 19–25)

That is the conclusion of Exodus 19. When we come to chapter 20, we read: "And God spoke all these words, saying: 'I am the LORD your God, who brought you out of the land of Egypt, out of the house of bondage. You shall have no other gods before Me'" (vv. 1–3). Then we get the rest of the Decalogue.

Again, the Ten Commandments do not appear here as the ground for the redemption of the people of Israel, for the people had already been redeemed by the sovereign, gracious work of God. The commandments are set forth in the context of God's national covenant with Israel. He had now called this people His people and said He would be their covenant Lord. He was constituting them as a nation—but not just any kind of a nation. The structure of this nation God was establishing was that of a theocracy.

We are familiar with words such as *democracy* and *monarchy*, even *oligarchy* and *plutocracy*. All of these are forms of government that have existed in various times and places throughout human history. By contrast, God's will for Israel was a theocracy, which is government by God Himself. God is the King of His people. The theocracy, in a sense, mirrors for us the concept of the kingdom of God, which also recognizes God as the supreme authority figure. The Ten Commandments, then, represent the basic structure, the ground rules, for this theocracy.

In the twentieth century, much attention was given to the structure of the ancient Near Eastern treaties, and scholars noted striking similarities to the covenant that God made with His people in Exodus 20. The ancient Near Eastern treaties, which were especially common among the Hittites, were called "suzerain-vassal treaties." The suzerain was the dominant king, while a vassal was a lesser party. Therefore, the suzerain had the power to exact oaths of loyalty from his vassals, and in return he would give them certain benefits and protection. He might give grain from his storehouses or promise that his armies would help support the vassals when they needed assistance. In return, the vassals would swear loyalty to the suzerain. So, these were not treaties of equals.

Typically, these treaties included certain elements. First, there was a preamble, in which the suzerain identified himself. He might say, "I, Hammurabi, king of the Yahabibi, king of the Hittites." Then there was a historical prologue, in which the suzerain would rehearse the benefits he had bestowed upon his vassals in the past: "I, Yahabibi, king of the Hittites, protected your daughters from the assault of the Amorites," or "I filled your barns with grain during the famine." Next were the stipulations of the treaty, that which the suzerain expected of the vassals and that which he pledged to do: "If you do such and such, I will do such and such." Also, the treaties spelled out sanctions or punishments that would be enacted if the terms of the treaty were violated. Finally, there were provisions for copies of the treaties for both parties, one for the suzerain and the other for the vassal, and provisions for public reading, from time to time, if the treaty had to be brought up to date.

It is not hard to see this literary structure in the Mosaic covenant. Exodus 20 begins with a preamble: "I am the LORD your God." Then there is a brief historical prologue: "who brought you out of the land of Egypt, out of the house of bondage." Here God reminds His people of the history of their relationship. Their God, their covenant Lord, is a personal God with a personal name and a personal history. That's so important for us in the Christian faith. We are not united by covenant to a nameless, amorphous force or some higher power; we are related to a covenant Lord who is personal. He has a name and a history in which He has worked for our redemption.

THE DECALOGUE

The third element of the covenant that I want to focus on, the Decalogue or the Ten Commandments, corresponds to the stipulations of the ancient Near Eastern treaties. Here God set forth His requirements for His people, beginning with the first commandment: "You shall have no other gods before Me."

These are the terms that God gave to His people, not so that they might enter into a covenant relationship with Him, but in order to stay in the covenant relationship, to retain that special privilege of grace they had received. God was saying, "I'm organizing you as My people." These are the terms of the theocratic state.

Notice that He did not give the terms of the theocratic state simply as an abstract ethical code, such as the Bill of Rights in the U.S. Constitution. Rather, the Decalogue that establishes the theocratic nation of Israel is profoundly religious and spiritual; in fact, almost the entire first half of the Decalogue is devoted to the people's spiritual obligations toward God. He tells them how to avoid idolatry, how to protect the sanctity of the name of God, how to celebrate the Sabbath, and so on. So, we see that there is a strong religious element in the theocracy.

I noted above that these stipulations are the basis not for their salvation, but for how they may remain in good standing with their covenant God. In history, we see the people becoming so apostate, grossly violating the commandments, that God sent them into exile and, as it were, divorced them for a time because they had committed spiritual harlotry. The law, then, is a way of manifesting one's loving obedience to the God who saves by grace. Likewise, in the New Testament, the new Mediator, Jesus, says to His disciples, who are not saved by their works but by His, "If you love Me, keep My commandments" (John 14:15).

The law also is given for a larger redemptive purpose, as the Apostle Paul unfolds for us in the New Testament. The law not only reveals the holiness of God, but it also is a mirror by which we see our lack of holiness. In this sense, the law does not stand in an antithetical relationship to the gospel; rather, it prefigures the gospel, because it is the schoolmaster that drives us to Christ. So, one of the most important functions of the law of God is to reveal to us our need for grace, our need for the gospel, our need for the Redeemer. It had that function then, just as it has now.

THE CEREMONIAL LAW

The fourth element of the Mosaic covenant that I want to highlight is the laws that are added later, after the Decalogue. We call these ritual laws because they have to do with the ceremonies, with the priesthood, the feasts, and how things function in the tabernacle. In all of these things, we see glorious anticipations of the redemption that is ours in Christ.

Two terms are used in discussions of the significance of the old covenant rituals: *symbol* and *type*. A symbol represents something other than itself, pointing beyond itself to a present reality. For example, the tabernacle symbolized the presence of God in the midst of the people. The tabernacle itself was not the presence of God. It was the tent of meeting, but as such, it called attention to God's promise to be with His people.

The word *type* comes from a word that originally had to do with making an imprint by striking something into a soft surface. The best illustration is the process of typing on a typewriter—the keys strike the paper, leaving an imprint. So, a type is a symbol of something future, something that reaches a greater fulfillment later on, and the New Testament tells us of various types and antitypes (fulfillments of types) from the Old Testament.

The tabernacle is not only a symbol of the presence of God, but also a type of the future presence of God in the incarnation. In other words, the tabernacle is a type of Jesus. In fact, Israel itself is a type of Christ. One of many parallels is the fact that just as Israel was delivered from Egypt, so Jesus was taken to Egypt as a baby to escape the murderous rampage of King Herod, and He was brought back to Israel by His parents only when God sent word by an angel (Matt. 2:13–15, 19–21). So, Matthew quoted Hosea 11:1, "Out of Egypt I called My Son" (Matt. 2:15), which originally applied to Israel, but he applied it to Jesus.

Typology is very tricky to interpret. Many times in the history of the church, scholars have developed highly allegorical ways of interpreting the Bible, seeing types in everything. For example, in the book of Joshua, we are told that Rahab hung a scarlet cord to mark her house for the conquering Israelites (Josh. 2:17–21). Some have said that the scarlet cord must represent the blood of Christ, which was the means of our redemption. There is no end to such speculation. The Bible draws no connection between the cord of Rahab and the blood of Christ, and it's dangerous for us to add to that.

However, we cannot deny that the New Testament, particularly the book of Hebrews, shows us that many things in the ceremonial law are intended to point beyond themselves. Again and again, the New Testament refers back to those ceremonies that reach their fulfillment and consummation in the ministry of Jesus. That's why the church no longer implements the Old Testament ceremonies; they were pointing beyond themselves to a future fulfillment, and once they were fulfilled, their use was ended.

All of the elements of the Mosaic covenant—the exodus, the covenant, the law, and the ceremonies—all point toward the gospel. They are not opposed to the gospel. They are not in place of the gospel. Rather, they are foundational to God's final revelation of the gospel.

CHAPTER 10

STUDY GUIDE

INTRODUCTION

During the time of Moses, the covenant made with Abraham had begun to see actual fulfill-ment. Every aspect of the Mosaic law was fulfilled in Christ Jesus, and every aspect pointed to Him. The Mosaic covenant was established *after* Israel's redemption from Egypt. Thus, it was a gracious covenant enacted to draw all the nations of the world to Israel's holy God. In this chapter, Dr. R. C. Sproul continues to expound upon the four major elements of the Mosaic covenant.

SCRIPTURE READINGS

Exodus 19–20; 24:1–8; Deuteronomy 7–8

LEARNING OBJECTIVE

To be able to summarize the most important elements of the Mosaic covenant, as well as how they relate to Scripture as a whole.

QUOTATION

And because you listen to these rules and keep and do them, the LORD your God will keep with you the covenant and the steadfast love that he swore to your fathers.... Take care lest your heart be deceived, and you turn aside and serve other gods and worship them; then the anger of the LORD will be kindled against you, and he will shut up the heavens, so that there will be no rain, and the land will yield no fruit, and you will perish quickly off the good land that the LORD is giving you.... It is not with you alone that I am making this sworn covenant, but with whoever is standing here with us today before the LORD our God, and with whoever is not here with us today.

—Deuteronomy 7:12; 11:16–17; 29:14—15

OUTLINE

I. First Element of the Mosaic Covenant: The Exodus (See previous chapter.)

II. Second Element of the Mosaic Covenant: The Making of the Mosaic Covenant

    A. The people swore allegiance to the covenant-maker (Exod. 24:1–8). Note that this was not an agreement between two equal parties. It was more like a pact made between a king and a vassal.

    B. At Mount Sinai, God recounted what He had done for them (Exod. 19:4). He then charged them to become sanctified (v. 10). Before the conditions of the covenant were given, the people had to be made clean.

    C. Two further points can be gleaned from this event:

        1. Expiation (the remission of sins): Wickedness had to be removed from the camp at Sinai before God could reveal His law (and by extension, Himself) to the people.

        2. The Ten Commandments were given in the midst of a national covenant. The commandments themselves were not conditions that, if met, would result in deliverance. No, God had already done that. Living out the law meant living a life of gratitude to God, as well as a means to draw all the surrounding nations to the one true God.

III. Third Element of the Mosaic Covenant: The Giving of the Law

    A. The giving of the law was to set up a theocracy in Israel. That is, God was to be their king. This is the covenantal aspect of the Decalogue that most resembles other ancient Near East treaties.

    B. In these ancient cultures, suzerains (kings) would make treaties with their vassals. This was very popular in the Hittite kingdom. The twentieth chapter of Exodus does share some similarities in its structure with these other nonbiblical treaties. They are as follows:

        1. Preamble (20:2a): "I am the LORD your God ..." The suzerain would identify himself and his stature to the people.

        2. Prologue (v. 2b): "... who brought you out of the land of Egypt, out of the house of slavery." The suzerain would then rehearse his shared history with the people and how he had taken care of them.

        3. Stipulations (vv. 3–17): "You shall have no other gods before me ..." The suzerain then spelled out the blessings that would come upon those who obeyed him and the curses that would befall those who disobeyed him.

        4. Public reading (24:7): The suzerain then confronted the people by reminding them of their obligations to him, and to update their shared history (as time went on). It also was a means to renew vows. We can see this happening throughout the Old Testament scriptures.

C. We must also remember that keeping the law was not salvific, for God had already delivered Israel. Obeying Him does not *earn* His favor, grace, or choice; rather, obeying sustains the covenant. That is, obedience keeps the people in covenant with God.

D. In the New Testament we see that the law is not a means for justification but for sanctification ("If you love me, you will keep my commandments" [John 14:15]). Paul spoke of the law as a tutor, or schoolmaster, who reveals to us our need for the gospel.

IV. Fourth Element of the Mosaic Covenant: The Ritual of the Law

A. In all the liturgy of the Mosaic covenant, we see a glorious anticipation of the new covenant.

B. Two terms are important for us to learn with respect to the foreshadowing of the Mosaic law:

1. Symbol: A symbol represents something beyond itself that is a present reality. For example, the tabernacle symbolized the presence of God. The tent itself was not *the* presence of God, but it pointed to His nearness to His people.

2. Type: A type refers to something in the future, which reaches a greater, or fuller, fulfillment in the thing to which the type refers (called an "antitype"). For example, the tabernacle is a type of the antitype Jesus. John wrote in the prologue to his gospel that

Jesus dwelled ("tabernacled") among us (see 1:14). In other words, the incarnation fulfilled in a greater way what the Old Testament tabernacle signified.

C. We see this type/antitype dialogue most often in the book of Hebrews. This is also why the church does not practice the Old Testament rituals, because they ended in redemptive history through the coming of the Messiah (since He fulfilled them all). No aspect of the Mosaic covenant is antithetical to the gospel (as some argue); rather, it prefigured and pointed to the gospel.

STUDY QUESTIONS

1. The making of the Mosaic covenant is like a pact _____.

    a. Made between kings

    b. Made between a king and a vassal

    c. Between two equal parties

    d. None of the above

2. At Mount Sinai, God recounted how He saved Israel; He then charged them to be sanctified. What does this convey?

    a. Expiation and the obedience to the law in gratitude, not for salvation

    b. That before the people may be set apart, purified, or made clean, they must be given the conditions of the covenant

    c. That before the conditions of the covenant are given, the people must be set apart, purified, or made clean

    d. Both a and c

3. Theocracy means _____.

    a. That a small group of holy people rule the nation

    b. That God is King, and that His laws are to be enforced in the land

    c. That God and a chosen king are equal rulers

    d. None of the above

4. The covenantal aspect of the Decalogue resembles which of the following?

    a. It does not resemble anything in the ancient world.

    b. Arabian sheikh treaties

    c. Persian satrap treaties

    d. Hittite suzerain-vassal treaties

5. Which of the following is not an aspect of the giving of the law?

    a. Preamble and prologue

    b. Bloodletting and idol worship

    c. Stipulations and public reading

    d. None of the above

6. Two major aspects of the ritual of the law are _____.

    a. Prophecy and dancing

    b. Eating raw meat and carving statues

c. Symbol and type

d. All of the above

DISCUSSION GUIDE

1. Search the Old Testament for the numerous references to the exodus event that describe it as *the* Old Testament redemption. How does this challenge the common opinion of many Christians that the Old Testament is irrelevant?

2. How are the themes of deliverance from bondage and sin, God's display of power and sovereign grace, and the Passover in the exodus from Egypt defining features of salvation as portrayed in *both* the Old and the New Testaments?

3. Read Exodus 19 and 24. In the making of the covenant between God and Israel, what was the great emphasis according to these texts (cf. 19:5, 8; 24:3)? Are the Israelites seen parleying with God about the nature and content of the covenant? Why not? What, then, was required of the people?

4. Reread Exodus 24:9–11, then 24:3–8. Now read Exodus 12:1–11. How do these events resemble the Passover, and how do they relate to biblical covenants?

5. The giving of the law, as mentioned in the chapter, served in one sense to organize the nation as a theocracy. What was this

theocracy to have looked like? What was it supposed to typify (point to, embody, anticipate)?

6. As pointed out, the law had been given *after* the redemption from Egypt had been accomplished, and the Israelites had already begun enjoying many of the blessings of the covenant. What, then, was the law for? From our standpoint in the new covenant, what is the law for? Have the purposes changed?

7. The ritual law is said to have prefigured the Messiah in many ways. Describe in your own words as many ways as you know of that the ceremonies of old typified the coming Christ. Include in your discussion the following: symbol and type, the tabernacle, and the sacrificial offerings.

SUGGESTED READING FOR FURTHER STUDY

Robertson, O. Palmer. *The Christ of the Covenants*, pp. 185–99
Vos, Geerhardus. *Biblical Theology: Old and New Testaments*, pp. 121–74

11

THE DAVIDIC COVENANT

I mentioned earlier that I believe the three most prominent figures in Old Testament history were Abraham, Moses, and David. It is interesting to me that God used each of these men as the mediator of a covenant. We have looked at the covenant with Abraham and the covenant with Moses. In this chapter, I want to consider the Davidic covenant, the covenant God made with King David. However, the roots of that covenant go much earlier than David himself, all the way back to the patriarchal period, to the final blessing Jacob gave to his sons as he was coming to the end of his life.

Jacob had twelve sons, the eldest son of whom was Reuben. As the firstborn, he normally would receive the heart of the patriarchal blessing, but because of his sins, Reuben was passed over, as were

Simeon and Levi, Jacob's second and third sons. Instead, the blessing went to Judah, Jacob's fourth son. Jacob said to Judah: "Judah, you are he whom your brothers shall praise; your hand shall be on the neck of your enemies; your father's children shall bow down before you. Judah is a lion's whelp; from the prey, my son, you have gone up. He bows down, he lies down as a lion; and as a lion, who shall rouse him?" (Gen. 49:8–9). Jacob referred to Judah as a lion. So, the title "the Lion of Judah" arose in Israel and became linked, ultimately, to the promised Messiah. We see this title applied to Jesus in Revelation 5:5.

Jacob continued, saying: "The scepter shall not depart from Judah, nor a lawgiver from between his feet, until Shiloh comes" (Gen. 49:10a). This reference to a scepter indicates kingship, because the scepter is a rod or wand, a symbol and sign of a king or ruler. Jacob, then, was prophesying that a king would come from the tribe of Judah. Jacob's statement that the scepter will not depart from Judah "until Shiloh comes" is a very difficult passage, and there is ongoing discussion as to what it means. It may refer to an event, such as the destruction of the sanctuary that was at Shiloh, or to a place, but no one is sure.

Continuing, Jacob said: "And to Him shall be the obedience of the people. Binding his donkey to the vine, and his donkey's colt to the choice vine, he washed his garments in wine, and his clothes in the blood of grapes. His eyes are darker than wine, and his teeth whiter than milk" (vv. 10b–12). So, we see that the favored status of the patriarchal blessing is passed to Judah.

That is significant for our consideration of the Davidic covenant, because David was the great king who descended from Judah, who became the head of the great dynasty in the Old Testament, which we see associated with all kinds of future promises about David's greater Son, who will come and bring the zenith of that kingdom. That greater Son, of course, is Christ.

A HOUSE FOR DAVID

We find the record of God's covenant with David in 2 Samuel 7. I find this chapter extremely interesting, partly because there is great irony in it. Samuel wrote: "Now it came to pass when the king was dwelling in his house, and the LORD had given him rest from all his enemies all around, that the king said to Nathan the prophet, 'See now, I dwell in a house of cedar, but the ark of God dwells inside tent curtains'" (vv. 1–2).

The king here is David, of course. He was now established in his reign and had built for himself a palace. One day, he said to the prophet Nathan: "What's wrong with this picture? Here I am, the king, and I have this magnificent house, this magnificent palace, but our God doesn't have a house. Instead, He has a tent that is transported here and there, and there's no permanency to that sanctuary. He deserves a magnificent temple." It was David's desire to build a magnificent house for God.

Samuel then told us:

> Then Nathan said to the king, "Go, do all that is in your heart, for the LORD is with you."

But it happened that night that the word of the LORD came to Nathan, saying, "Go and tell My servant David, 'Thus says the LORD: "Would you build a house for Me to dwell in? For I have not dwelt in a house since the time that I brought the children of Israel up from Egypt, even to this day, but have moved about in a tent and in a tabernacle. Wherever I have moved about with all the children of Israel, have I ever spoken a word to anyone from the tribes of Israel, whom I commanded to shepherd My people Israel, saying, 'Why have you not built Me a house of cedar?'"' Now therefore, thus shall you say to My servant David, 'Thus says the LORD of hosts: "I took you from the sheepfold, from following the sheep, to be ruler over My people, over Israel. And I have been with you wherever you have gone, and have cut off all your enemies from before you, and have made you a great name, like the name of the great men who are on the earth. Moreover I will appoint a place for My people Israel, and will plant them, that they may dwell in a place of their own and move no more; nor shall the sons of wickedness oppress them anymore, as previously, since the time that I commanded judges to be over My people Israel, and have caused you to rest from

all your enemies. Also the LORD tells you that
He will make you a house.""" (vv. 3–11)

At this point in time, Israel was still getting settled in the Promised Land. They had been a nomadic people with no permanent place to call their own. Was God going to continue to "dwell" in a tent? Were the people going to continue to wander with a portable sanctuary, or would there be a fixed, permanent central sanctuary that would have longevity and perpetual significance to the people? That is what this discussion is about. God answered by promising to appoint a place for the people and plant them there.

Then God made a startling promise to David. Nathan said, "Also the LORD tells you that He will make you a house." Here is the first and most important ingredient of the Davidic covenant. God said, "I never asked you to build Me a house." As we know, He did not give that opportunity to David, but bestowed it on his son Solomon, who then built the temple in Jerusalem. But the terms of the covenant with David did include a house. David wanted to build a dwelling place for God, but God said no. Instead, God promised to build a house for David. Of course, David already had a magnificent cedar palace. But God was not talking about a home. The house that God was promising David was a dynasty. He was promising dynastic succession to the sons of David.

In antiquity, dynasties were extremely important to royalty. In the ancient Near East, for example, Egypt had several dynasties. But in all of the history of Egypt, the longest dynasty was 250 years. Likewise, when the northern kingdom of Israel split away from Judah during the reign of Solomon's son Rehoboam, a succession of dynasties held the throne, but the longest was about 100 years. In contrast to these dynasties, the dynasty of David lasted for 400 years, which, just on the human plane of history, is an extremely remarkable phenomenon. However, considering that the David dynasty was a "house" that God built, its longevity is no surprise at all.

Nathan, speaking the words of God, went on to say:

> When your days are fulfilled and you rest with your fathers, I will set up your seed after you, who will come from your body, and I will establish his kingdom. He shall build a house for My name, and I will establish the throne of his kingdom forever. I will be his Father, and he shall be My son. If he commits iniquity, I will chasten him with the rod of men and with the blows of the sons of men. But My mercy shall not depart from him, as I took it from Saul, whom I removed from before you. And your house and your kingdom shall be established forever before you. Your throne shall be established forever. (vv. 12–16)

God here was speaking of Solomon. He would build the temple, God said. But God said that Solomon not only would be David's son, but he would be God's "son." So, added to the idea of a dynasty is the concept that the Davidic kings were "sons of God."

They were adopted into the family of God so that each king in the line of David had this special designation as a son to God—not the Son of God in the supreme theological sense that Jesus is, but one in an intimate relationship with God. Furthermore, God said, this relationship is going to last forever. This pointed clearly to David's greater Son, who was not only David's Son but also David's Lord.

THE LORD'S ANOINTED

Psalm 2 is very important as a messianic psalm written by David. It begins with a question: "Why do the nations rage, and the people plot a vain thing? The kings of the earth set themselves, and the rulers take counsel together, against the LORD and against His Anointed" (vv. 1–2). The idea here was a summit meeting of all of the rulers of the world, and the purpose of their meeting was to draw up a strategy to overthrow the king of the Jews. The word *Anointed* is the term from which we get the Greek word *Christos*, or "Christ." In the first instance, the anointed king is David. He was a type of Christ, who was to come. At this summit meeting, the pagan rulers came together and said, "Let us break Their bonds in pieces and cast away Their cords from us" (v. 3). So, this is a conspiracy to rebel against the authority of God and against His anointed Son.

The response of God to this scenario is this: "He who sits in the heavens shall laugh; the LORD shall hold them in derision" (v. 4). God looks down from heaven, sees all the assembled power and might of the kings of this world who are aiming their guns at His

Messiah, and God laughs. But not for long. "Then He shall speak to them in His wrath, and distress them in His deep displeasure: 'Yet, I have set My King on My holy hill of Zion'" (vv. 5–6).

The psalm then says: "I will declare the decree: The LORD has said to Me, 'You are My Son, today I have begotten You. Ask of Me, and I will give You the nations for Your inheritance, and the ends of the earth for Your possession'" (vv. 7–8). Again, the initial application of this psalm is David, but its greater application, its messianic application, is Christ, before whom all of the kingdoms of the world rise up in an adversarial posture, trying to overthrow Him as the King of the kings, which is an exercise in futility because God has established His Son as King forever.

Even though David's dynasty lasted four hundred years, it was troubled almost from the very beginning. King Solomon was not faithful to the covenant. We read in Scripture:

> But King Solomon loved many foreign women, as well as the daughter of Pharaoh: women of the Moabites, Ammonites, Edomites, Sidonians, and Hittites—from the nations of whom the LORD had said to the children of Israel, "You shall not intermarry with them, nor they with you. Surely they will turn away your hearts after their gods." Solomon clung to these in love. And he had seven hundred wives, princesses, and three hundred concubines; and his wives turned away his heart. For it was so, when Solomon was old, that his

wives turned his heart after other gods; and his
heart was not loyal to the LORD his God, as was
the heart of his father David. For Solomon went
after Ashtoreth the goddess of the Sidonians, and
after Milcom the abomination of the Ammonites.
Solomon did evil in the sight of the LORD, and
did not fully follow the LORD, as did his father
David. (1 Kings 11:1–6)

Not surprisingly, God was angry with Solomon for this
unfaithfulness. As we read on, we see God's stern response:

So the LORD became angry with Solomon,
because his heart had turned from the LORD God
of Israel, who had appeared to him twice, and
had commanded him concerning this thing, that
he should not go after other gods; but he did not
keep what the LORD had commanded. Therefore
the LORD said to Solomon, "Because you have
done this, and have not kept My covenant and
My statutes, which I have commanded you, I will
surely tear the kingdom away from you and give
it to your servant. Nevertheless I will not do it
in your days, for the sake of your father David; I
will tear it out of the hand of your son. However I
will not tear away the whole kingdom; I will give
one tribe to your son for the sake of My servant

David, and for the sake of Jerusalem which I have
chosen." (vv. 9–13)

What follows is the radical division of the kingdom. But
throughout the period of the divided kingdom, there was always
a Davidic king on the throne, until the ultimate collapse of that
kingship in the Babylonian captivity. At that point, it seemed as if
God's promise of an everlasting Davidic kingdom had failed after
only four hundred years, and there was an interim when there was
no son of David on the throne in Jerusalem. But the prophet Amos
gave the word of God to the people, saying, "I will raise up the tabernacle of David, which has fallen down, and repair its damages; I
will raise up its ruins, and rebuild it as in the days of old" (9:11).
Beyond the exile would come the establishment of the ultimate
Davidic king, who, indeed, will reign forever. And we'll look at
that in the next chapter.

CHAPTER 11

STUDY GUIDE

INTRODUCTION

As biblical history continued to unfold, so too did God's revelation through covenants. To be sure, it gets more complex, but also much fuller when revealing God's glory. In this chapter, Dr. R. C. Sproul discusses the Davidic covenant—its patriarchal roots, its promises, and its messianic themes.

SCRIPTURE READINGS

2 Samuel 7; 2 Chronicles 6:12–42

LEARNING OBJECTIVE

To be able to summarize the most important elements of the Davidic covenant and how they relate to Scripture as a whole.

QUOTATION

Thus says the LORD of hosts, I took you from the pasture, from following the sheep, that you should be prince over my people Israel.... And I will make for you a great name, like the name of the great ones of the earth.... And I will give you rest from all your enemies. Moreover, the LORD declares to you that the LORD will make you a house. When your days are fulfilled and you lie down with your fathers, I will raise up your offspring after you, who shall come from your body, and I will establish his kingdom. He shall build a house for my name, and I will establish the throne of his kingdom forever.... When he commits iniquity, I will discipline him... but my steadfast love will not depart from him.... And your house and your kingdom shall be made sure forever before me. Your throne shall be established forever.

—2 Samuel 7:8–9, 11–16

OUTLINE

I. Patriarchal Roots of the Davidic Covenant

A. In Jacob's prophetic blessing of his twelve sons in Genesis 49, we see the patriarch pass over Reuben, Simeon, and Levi and give Judah the ultimate blessing.

B. He called Judah (whose name means "praised"; cf. 29:35) a "lion's cub" (v. 9). Note that the phrase "Lion of the tribe of Judah" finds its origins here.

C. In verse 10, Jacob said that "the scepter shall not depart from Judah," which signifies that royalty will come from this tribe (cf. 2 Sam. 7:16). This dynasty should not depart, Jacob added, "until tribute comes to him." Other versions of the Bible render this phrase "until he comes to whom it belongs," "until Shiloh comes," and "until he comes to Shiloh." Whatever the absolute meaning, all interpretations see this phrase as referring to the Davidic covenant, and quite possibly to the coming of the King greater than David.

II. God's Covenant with David: 2 Samuel 7

A. David, a skilled military leader and diplomat, sought to unite the people of Israel by moving the capital city from Shiloh (located in the heart of the northern kingdom) to a more neutral location—Jerusalem. David intended to build God a sanctuary, and God's prophet, Nathan, gave his blessing.

B. But God called on Nathan to speak His word to the king and declare the terms of the covenant. Regarding David's initial desire to build a sanctuary for the Lord, God responded in the negative. On the contrary, God would build David a house—not one made of cedar, but a dynasty. David's royal line did last a long time in comparison to other dynasties in history (400 years compared to the northern kingdom's 100 years and Egypt's 250 years). A spiritual aspect was also added to the political establishment of the Davidic throne: the kings would serve mediatorial roles in the theocracy as "sons of God." This pointed beyond itself to the perpetual kingdom of the Lion of Judah Himself.

III. Sonship

A. In Psalm 2, a "messianic" psalm, the king cries out against the rulers of the world who have gathered together to plot against the Lord and His anointed (in Greek, the word is *Christos*).

B. He also wrote that the Lord has set His king on the holy hill of Zion (v. 6). While this has primary reference to the Davidic king, it has a greater application to the Christ, the King of Kings.

C. In 2 Samuel 7:14–16 we see the sin of Solomon referenced (cf. 1 Kings 11:1ff.). As a result of Solomon's turning away, God tore the kingdom from him, but not in his lifetime, "for the sake of David [his] father" (1 Kings 11:12).

D. In the end, David's throne did indeed fall. What, then, of God's promise? The prophet Amos addressed this directly: "In that day I will raise up the booth of David that is fallen and repair its breaches, and raise up its ruins and rebuild it as in the days of old" (9:11).

E. From this restoration onward, the Davidic throne would endure forever. Thus, we see once again that the predictions and psalms of old pointed through their original meanings to the coming Messiah, who would reestablish God's kingdom on earth.

STUDY QUESTIONS

1. In what book and chapter of the Bible does Jacob bless his twelve sons?

    a. 2 Samuel 7

    b. Genesis 49

    c. Deuteronomy 33

    d. Genesis 27

2. What did he predict about the line of Judah?

    a. That royalty shall come from his older brother's tribe

    b. That royalty shall come from his tribe

    c. That the priesthood shall come from his tribe

    d. That a great prophet shall come from his tribe

3. To which of David's offers did God respond in the negative?

    a. His offer to move the ark to Shiloh

    b. His offer to build the temple in Jerusalem

    c. His offer to provide the northern tribes security

    d. His offer to build a synagogue in Jerusalem

4. What was God's counteroffer?

    a. God would build the temple Himself.

    b. God would repeal His covenant with Moses.

    c. God would make a dynasty out of David's family.

    d. None of the above

5. Which king was greater than David?

    a. Solomon

    b. Jehoshaphat

    c. Asa

    d. Jesus

6. At the time of the restoration of the Davidic throne, the prophets declared _____.

    a. That David would be reincarnated and rule once again

    b. That its longevity depended on the people's response

    c. That the reestablishment would last until the Messiah came

    d. That it would never end

DISCUSSION GUIDE

1. While the word for covenant (*berîyth*) is not used in the portion of Scripture that describes God's dealings with David, how do the following passages describe this event? How do these passages serve to bind the Davidic covenant to the other covenants of God's progressing revelation (2 Sam. 23:5; Pss. 89:3; 132:11–12)?

2. Read 2 Samuel 5:6–7; 6:1–2, 7b; 7:1. What three events are described here? How were they used in God's providence to prepare the way for His covenant with David? With an eye on eschatology, how did this scenario anticipate the last days, the kingdom of peace?

3. Read 2 Samuel 7:5 and 11. Describe the situation and how God played on the word *house*. What was God promising David? Read 2 Samuel 5:3. How does being a king in this theocracy parallel the prophet and priest roles in covenant mediating?

4. Read 2 Samuel 7:14. How is the relationship between the earthly king and the heavenly King described? Why is this significant (cf. Ps. 2:7; Isa. 9:6; Rom. 1:3–4; Heb. 1:5)?

5. Did the Davidic covenant flow out of the Mosaic or Abrahamic covenant? Does it have to be "either/or"? Why or why not? Include in the answer your understanding of biblical revelation and how it unfolds (progressively or otherwise).

6. Read 1 Kings 2:1–4; 9:4–5. Did David see this covenant God had made with him as a supplanting covenant over the one established at Mount Sinai?

7. The biblical history of the Israelite nation from the time of the Davidic covenant onward is not pretty. Through apostasy, the nation was finally exiled from the Promised Land. But read 2 Kings 25:27–30 and 2 Chronicles 36:22–23. Why, in the midst of covenant curses, is there this glimmer of hope? How, then, does the Davidic covenant parallel themes from both the Abrahamic and the Mosaic covenants?

SUGGESTED READING FOR FURTHER STUDY

Robertson, O. Palmer. *The Christ of the Covenants*, pp. 229–69

12

THE NEW COVENANT (PART 1)

The new covenant is not something that comes out of the blue; it is intimately related to the covenants that went before it. Nevertheless, there are new elements that stand in contrast to those of the previous covenants, yet all of these earlier covenants look beyond themselves to the future consummation of the promises that are contained within them. All those promises are fulfilled under the terms of the new covenant.

The prophet Jeremiah was given a vision of the new covenant:

Behold, the days are coming, says the LORD, when I will make a new covenant with the house of Israel and with the house of Judah—not according to the covenant that I made with their fathers in the day that I took them by the hand to lead them out of the land of Egypt, My covenant which they broke, though I was a husband to them, says the LORD. But this is the covenant that I will make with the house of Israel after those days, says the LORD: I will put My law in their minds, and write it on their hearts; and I will be their God, and they shall be My people. No more shall every man teach his neighbor, and every man his brother, saying, "Know the LORD," for they all shall know Me, from the least of them to the greatest of them, says the LORD. For I will forgive their iniquity, and their sin I will remember no more. (31:31–34)

The terms of this covenant, as they are listed in this text, are a little bit problematic. We're not exactly sure what God meant when He said, "I will forgive their iniquity." We understand, according to the New Testament books of Hebrews and Romans, that salvation is the same in the Old Testament and the New Testament. The Holy Spirit operated in the hearts of people in the Old Testament. He regenerated people in the Old Testament. Justification was by faith in the Old Testament, just as it is in the New Testament. We also see that people's sins were forgiven in the Old Testament. So why did God specify that sins would be forgiven under the new covenant?

It is a difference in degree, I think. That's why I say the new covenant grows out of the old covenant, and there is no radical discontinuity between them. But, as the author of Hebrews told us, the new covenant is a greater covenant, a better covenant (7:22). It's not enough to call it the new covenant because the new covenant is the final covenant. It is the covenant of completion, the covenant of consummation, which all of the other covenants point toward.

We know people in Old Testament times had forgiveness of sins. Forgiveness was symbolized and typified in the feasts, in the sacrificial system, and especially on the Day of Atonement. But the Day of Atonement was an annual event; it had to be repeated every year. Likewise, the sacrifices and offerings had to be performed over and over again. But in the new covenant, the sacrifice is made once for all, so that the remission of sins for the people of God is accomplished forever. The whole ceremonial system of the Old Testament came to a screeching halt when all of its symbolism was fulfilled in the ministry of Christ. Therefore, I think what we see in the promise made through Jeremiah is the greater fulfillment of the principles that were set forth in the Old Testament covenants.

THE KINGDOM OF HEAVEN

The New Testament opens with the appearance of John the Baptist, coming from the wilderness and calling the people to repentance.

He arrived at a decisive moment in history. In my opinion, John the Baptist is the most underappreciated character in the New Testament, because what John did is absolutely radical. The voice of prophecy in Israel had been silenced for four hundred years, since the close of the Old Testament canon with the prophecies of Malachi. Then John suddenly appeared, behaving very much like the ancient prophet Elijah. However, he introduced a requirement to the Jews that was never a part of their covenant requirements in antiquity.

In the intertestamental period, the Jews developed the practice of proselyte baptism for Gentiles who wanted to become Jews. In order to become Jews, Gentiles had to make a profession of faith in Judaism, be circumcised, and undergo a ritual bath of purification because the Gentiles were considered to be unclean. They were strangers to the covenants (Eph. 2:12). But then John appeared and called the Jews to undergo this bath.

The Jewish officials in Jerusalem were outraged by this. They were the children of Abraham, God's chosen people. What need did they have to be purified? John's response, basically, was "Because you're unclean." They needed to be baptized as a sign of repentance from sin because the breakthrough of the kingdom of God, the fulfillment of all the prophecies in the earlier covenants, was imminent. "Repent," John said, "for the kingdom of heaven is at hand!" (Matt. 3:2). No longer was the kingdom some far off, mysterious future event; it was about to happen. John said, "Even now the ax is laid to the root of the trees" and "His winnowing fan is in His hand" (Matt. 3:10, 12), two metaphors that communicate the imminence of the kingdom's coming. The coming of the kingdom of God meant a new dimension of the reign of God. It meant that the fallen house of David was about to be righted and reestablished.

When Jesus began His public ministry, His message was the same: "Repent, for the kingdom of God is at hand" (Matt. 4:17). Later, however, He said, "The kingdom of God is within you" (Luke 17:21b). I think that's a very poor translation. It's a possible translation because of the Greek, but it gives the idea that the kingdom of God is an ethereal, spiritual thing that occurs in the hearts of people. That's not what Jesus was saying. A better translation is, "The kingdom of God is among you; it's in your midst." So, Jesus preached what Matthew calls "the gospel of the kingdom" (4:23).

What is the gospel of Christ? The good news that Jesus announced was not directly the gospel of Jesus Christ. When Paul talked about the gospel, he talked about the gospel of Jesus Christ. This is the gospel, the good news about Jesus, and it rehearses all the things that Jesus accomplished in our behalf. But when the term *gospel* was used by Jesus or in reference to Jesus, it referred to the gospel of the kingdom. It was the good news that the long-awaited messianic kingdom was arriving. All we need to do is look at Jesus' parables and ask ourselves what they are about. The overwhelming majority of the parables focus on one concept: the kingdom of God. In many of His parables, Jesus said, "The kingdom of heaven is like …" He was clarifying it for the people.

At the same time, Jesus was very secretive about using the term *Messiah*, because He knew that the people of His day had a completely distorted concept of what the Messiah was to be. The one thing they could not imagine was a messiah who was a Shepherd-King and also a suffering servant. The disciples were horrified when Jesus told them that He had to go to Jerusalem to lay down His life for His people. They could not understand it. Peter gave his great confession at Caesarea Philippi when Jesus asked, "Who do men say that I, the Son of Man, am?" Peter replied, "You are the Christ, the Son of the living God." For that confession, Jesus blessed him by saying, "Blessed are you, Simon Bar-Jonah, for flesh and blood has not revealed this to you, but My Father who is in heaven. And I also say to you that you are Peter, and on this rock I will build My church" (Matt. 16:13b–18a). But what seems to be only a few minutes later, Jesus told the disciples that He had to go to Jerusalem to suffer and die. Peter said, "Far be it from You, Lord; this shall not happen to You!" (v. 22). At that, Jesus said, "Get behind Me, Satan! You are an offense to Me" (v. 23). The one whom Jesus called Peter now received a different nickname—Satan. Even the disciples did not understand the way in which the fulfillment of all the covenants would take place.

There are many similarities between Jesus and Moses. We saw that Moses was the mediator of the old covenant, and Jesus is the Mediator of the new covenant. Moses was the great prophet of antiquity. And yet, Moses himself prophesied that God would raise up "a Prophet like me" (Deut. 18:15). That prophecy was fulfilled in Christ, who is the supreme Prophet of all Scripture. He's both the object and the subject of prophecy. When He spoke about future events, He spoke about Himself.

Not only is He the Great Prophet, but He also performs the work of the Great High Priest. He comes as a Priest, not of the Aaronic priesthood, but the priesthood of Melchizedek. He is also the supreme King. He is David's greater Son, who, at the same time, is David's Lord. That's why Psalm 110 is so important to the New Testament. In that psalm, David said, under the inspiration of the Holy Spirit, "The LORD said to my Lord, 'Sit at My right hand'" (v. 1). David was acknowledging that God was apportioning a position of authority to One who is David's Lord. That is why we see this line between David to Jesus and the fulfilling of the Davidic covenant in Christ in the New Testament.

THE INAUGURATION OF THE COVENANT

One of the questions people often ask about the new covenant is "When does it start?" We see the announcement of the coming kingdom during the ministry of Jesus, but the actual making of the covenant, I think, took place in the upper room on the night when Jesus was betrayed. Luke tells us:

> When the hour had come, He sat down, and the twelve apostles with Him. Then He said to them, "With fervent desire I have desired to eat this Passover with you before I suffer; for I say to you,

I will no longer eat of it until it is fulfilled in the kingdom of God."

Then He took the cup, and gave thanks, and said, "Take this and divide it among yourselves; for I say to you, I will not drink of the fruit of the vine until the kingdom of God comes."

And He took bread, gave thanks and broke it, and gave it to them, saying, "This is My body which is given for you; do this in remembrance of Me." Likewise He also took the cup after supper, saying, "This cup is the new covenant in My blood, which is shed for you." (22:14–20)

Jesus and His disciples were celebrating the Passover, the liturgy that remembered the night when God brought vengeance against the children of the Egyptians, but passed over the houses of God's people who had smeared the blood of lambs on their doorposts. God had commanded that the people remember that and celebrate it on an annual basis. And so, Jesus, being a Jew, celebrated the Passover. In fact, because He knew He was about to die, He was eager to celebrate it with His disciples. But in the middle of the liturgy, He suddenly changed it. He said that the bread represented His body and that the wine represented His blood, and He pronounced a new covenant. That's when I believe the new covenant was initiated.

The next day, I think, Jesus ratified the covenant when He shed His blood on the cross. It is a new covenant for all who are in Christ, who participate in Him, who are the benefactors of His perfect, once-for-all sacrifice.

The story does not end with the ratification ceremony at Golgotha. The fact that this new covenant was firmly established and received the supreme blessing of God is shown by the resurrection. The New Testament tells us that "it was not possible that He should be held by [death]" (Acts 2:24), for He knew no sin. And after the resurrection, He sojourned on the earth for a few weeks with His disciples until He ascended into heaven. What is the point of the ascension? "No one has ascended to heaven but He who came down from heaven, that is, the Son of Man who is in heaven" (John 3:13). Jesus was not saying that no one else ever went to heaven. Enoch went to heaven. Abraham went to heaven. Many people, we suppose, have gone to heaven. But *ascension* carries a technical meaning, for it has to do not simply with going up, but going up to a specific place for a specific purpose. Jesus went to the right hand of God, and the purpose for His ascent was to go to His coronation, His investiture, as the fulfillment of the Davidic covenant. God crowned Him, not just as one more king in the line of Davidic kings, but as the King of Kings and the Lord of Lords, to whom all the nations of the world are given. His reign was announced by God in the new covenant, not to last for four hundred years, like the dynasty of David, but forever and ever, to which the church cries, "Hallelujah!"

In our day, many people think of the kingdom of God as something in the future. Yes, there's still another chapter to be written. Yes, there's still to be a consummation. Yes, the kingdom is now invisible. And yes, there will be a time when our reigning King will make His kingdom visible. But it already has come in terms of its inauguration. It's real, right now. Every time we come together at the Lord's Table, we're not just looking back to His death, but also to His return. We're at the table of the King, where we've been invited to sit down with the One who has sat down at the right hand of God in the kingdom. With that is the promise that we also will sit with Him and reign with Him in the final consummation of that kingdom.

CHAPTER 12

STUDY GUIDE

INTRODUCTION

In this the first of three chapters on the new covenant, we look at the summing up of the old covenant in the work of one man: John the Baptist. How are we to understand his baptism? How does his work as the forerunner of Jesus relate to the theme of biblical covenants? In this chapter, Dr. R. C. Sproul explores the ministry of the Baptizer and his relationship to the new covenant.

SCRIPTURE READINGS

Jeremiah 31:27–40; Hebrews 8

LEARNING OBJECTIVE

To understand how the new covenant relates to all the previous covenants portrayed in Scripture.

QUOTATIONS

For when I have brought them into the land flowing with milk and honey, which I swore to give to their fathers, and they have eaten and are full and grown fat, they will turn to other gods and serve them, and despise me and break my covenant.... Behold, the days are coming, declares the LORD, when I will make a new covenant with the house of Israel and the house of Judah, not like the covenant that I made with their fathers on the day when I took them by the hand to bring them out of the land of Egypt, my covenant that they broke, though I was their husband, declares the LORD.

—Deuteronomy 31:20; Jeremiah 31:31–32

OUTLINE

I. The New Covenant

A. All of the previous covenants pointed beyond themselves to the new covenant of Christ Jesus.

B. Ezekiel's preaching pointed to the future restoration of the people of God.

C. Jeremiah 31 speaks of the new covenant as growing out of the old covenant. While there is nothing new about sins being forgiven (v. 34), the difference is in degrees. The new covenant, which will bring forgiveness of sins, will bring remission *once and for all* (cf. Heb. 10).

II. The Ministry of John the Baptizer

A. How are we to understand John's baptism? During the intertestamental period (lasting approximately four hundred years), the baptizing of proselytes (converts to Judaism) became a regular practice.

B. This is John's baptism. The irony was that John was calling those who were already ethnically part of Israel. By charging them to repent and be baptized, he was saying that despite their ethnic heritage they were still unclean outsiders to the covenant. No wonder his ministry was met with skepticism from the religious elite. By John's time, the kingdom of God was at hand (the ax was laid at the root), so his baptizing also served as an announcement of the restoration of the kingdom through the Anointed One.

C. Jesus taught much the same thing regarding the kingdom: "The kingdom of God is in the midst of you," He said to the Pharisees (Luke 17:21). God's kingdom, according to Jesus, had broken into history, and the Davidic throne was beginning to be reestablished—this time for all eternity. The messianic kingdom has come (cf. the "kingdom" parables of Jesus).

D. But the people generally had a poor understanding of how the kingdom was to take shape. They overemphasized one aspect (the military aspect) at the expense of the others (that their sins needed to be atoned for). This is why at times we see Jesus referring to Himself as the "Son of Man" over against the loftier title of "Messiah," for their views of the Messiah were distorted—they had no idea of the suffering He had to undergo. Even the Apostle Peter misunderstood this (Mark 8:33).

E. Moses was a type of Christ since he was the great mediating prophet in the old covenant. But Jesus was both the subject and the object of spoken (Old Testament) prophecy. Also, the Aaronic priesthood was superseded by Jesus' priesthood, which is after the order of Melchizedek. Finally, Jesus was the supreme King (cf. Ps. 10). David was also a type of Christ, and he typified Jesus, who was the greater, everlasting King.

III. When Did the New Covenant Begin?

A. Quite possibly, it began in the upper room, when our Lord spoke the words of institution: "This cup that is poured out for you is the new covenant in my blood" (Luke 22:20).

B. In the above verse, Jesus changed the liturgy of the Passover meal. The blood that was poured out was the blood of the lamb on the doorpost. But in the middle of this supper, Jesus said in effect that His body and blood took the place of the sacrificial lamb—only this time it is perpetually beneficial, that is, the sacrifice was enacted once and for all time.

C. This new covenant was ratified on the cross. But it did not end there, for Jesus rose from the dead and then ascended, two events that must inform our views of these last days. The ascension was not just a mere "going up"; it was a coronation not of just another Davidic king, but of the King of Kings.

D. Thus, the kingdom of God has already come. To be sure, there are elements that have yet to be fulfilled. This is why during Holy Communion we celebrate not just Jesus' redemptive death but His ascension (to be understood as synonymous with His everlasting session as the victorious King at the right hand of the Father).

STUDY QUESTIONS

1. What is so new about the new covenant?

    a. God became three in one.

    b. The new covenant is for children, too.

    c. Sins are forgiven *once and for all.*

    d. None of the above

2. John's baptism signified _____.

    a. That the kingdom of God had already come

    b. The inclusion of the outsider into the kingdom of God

    c. That the kingdom of God was yet a long way off

    d. None of the above

3. Messianic expectations in the first century _____.

    a. Underemphasized the military role of the Messiah

    b. Virtually ignored the need for a perfect atonement

    c. Were balanced and God honoring

    d. Overemphasized the fact that the Messiah needed to suffer

4. Why was Jesus a greater prophet than Moses?

    a. He was born in Bethlehem.

    b. He spoke prophetically, and He was Himself the subject of prophecy.

    c. Because He was baptized by John the Baptist.

    d. All of the above

5. What took the place of the Old Testament sacrificial lamb?

    a. Each of our own sufferings do.

    b. Jesus' body and blood

    c. Both a and b

    d. None of the above

6. The ascension of Jesus is synonymous with _____.

    a. His going up to heaven in order to wait to rule

    b. His coronation as the cosmic King of all creation

    c. His everlasting session as the victorious King at the Father's right hand

    d. Both b and c

DISCUSSION GUIDE

1. Read Matthew 11:14 and 17:10–13. What does the "if you are willing to accept it" statement by Jesus in 11:14 suggest? Could there have been some people who doubted that John was Elijah?

2. Now read John 1:21. How are we to explain this seeming contradiction? What misconception might John have been challenging in this passage? In what way, then, was John Elijah, and in what way was he not Elijah?

3. Read Matthew 3:2, 12 and Luke 3:9. How does the pivotal phrase, "Repent, for the kingdom of heaven is at hand" relate to John's role as the forerunner of the Messiah? How does it recapitulate the entire Old Testament (hint: law and prophecy)? Why does he call people to "repent" *before* "the kingdom of heaven" comes? If nothing else, then, what does the coming of this kingdom signify (remember the winnowing fork [Matt. 3:12] and the ax [Luke 3:9])?

4. In general, should the baptism of John (Mark 1:4) and the baptism of Christ (Matt. 28:19; cf. Acts 19:2–6) be separated? Are there any Scripture passages that suggest that those who came from John were baptized again when they came to Christ? So, then, do you think that the disciples of John in Acts 19 were rebaptized (with water)?

5. Read Matthew 3:11; Mark 1:4; and Luke 3:3. What is the expected result of the act of baptism? What was its *purpose*? If baptism actually

produces something, can it be a mere symbol? How does this challenge or confirm your opinions about baptism as a true conveyor of grace?

6. Still, are the baptism of John and the Christian sacrament one and the same? Why or why not? During the time of the Reformation, two extreme views ruled the day: the Catholics held that John's baptism was a mere sign, a type of that which was to come, while most Protestants held that the two baptisms were not to be distinquished. Is there a middle approach? What, if anything, did John's baptism *not* convey (cf. Matt. 3:11)? What significant event in church history after the ascension of Jesus conjoins baptism with the Holy Spirit?

7. Read Matthew 3:13–15. What does this passage (esp. v. 14) say about Jesus' character? If the goal of John's baptism was the repentance of sinners/forgiveness of sins, why did Jesus subject Himself to it? Include in your answer how Jesus as *the* Israel identified with the nation through this act.

SUGGESTED READING FOR FURTHER STUDY

Robertson, O. Palmer. *The Christ of the Covenants,* pp. 271–78
Vos, Geerhardus. *Biblical Theology: Old and New Testaments,* pp. 311–29

13

THE NEW COVENANT (PART 2)

Much of the book of Hebrews is devoted to comparing and contrasting the superiority of Jesus over Old Testament counterparts such as the priests, the tabernacle, the sacrifices, and so on. In the midst of this analysis of the superiority of Christ, we see also a study of the superiority of the new covenant over the old covenant.

The unknown author of Hebrews wrote:

> For every high priest is appointed to offer both
> gifts and sacrifices. Therefore it is necessary that
> this One also have something to offer. For if He

> were on earth, He would not be a priest, since there are priests who offer the gifts according to the law; who serve the copy and shadow of the heavenly things, as Moses was divinely instructed when he was about to make the tabernacle. For He said, "See that you make all things according to the pattern shown you on the mountain." But now He has obtained a more excellent ministry, inasmuch as He is also Mediator of a better covenant, which was established on better promises. (8:3–6)

This is a qualitative description of the new covenant as a better covenant. It's not only newer; it's better. It is declared to be better initially because it has a better Mediator and better promises than the old covenant. Furthermore, the words *copy* and *shadow* show that the ceremonies of the old covenant were types; that is, they pointed beyond themselves to the future. They were shadows of the full reality that was to come later.

Then, expanding on the superiority of the new covenant, the author went on to say:

> For if that first covenant had been faultless, then no place would have been sought for a second. Because finding fault with them, He says: "Behold, the days are coming, says the LORD, when I will make a new covenant with the house of Israel and with the house of Judah—not according to the

covenant that I made with their fathers in the day when I took them by the hand to lead them out of the land of Egypt; because they did not continue in My covenant, and I disregarded them, says the LORD. For this is the covenant that I will make with the house of Israel after those days, says the LORD: I will put My laws in their mind and write them on their hearts; and I will be their God, and they shall be My people. None of them shall teach his neighbor, and none his brother, saying, 'Know the LORD,' for all shall know Me, from the least of them to the greatest of them. For I will be merciful to their unrighteousness, and their sins and their lawless deeds I will remember no more."

In that He says, "A new covenant," He has made the first obsolete. Now what is becoming obsolete and growing old is ready to vanish away. (vv. 7–13)

Here the author quoted the lengthy prophecy from Jeremiah 31 that we considered in the previous chapter. However, he noted that when God spoke of a new covenant, He was saying that the old covenant was obsolete.

In Hebrews 9, we read of the first aspect of the fulfillment:

Then indeed, even the first covenant had ordinances of divine service and the earthly sanctuary.

For a tabernacle was prepared: the first part, in which was the lampstand, the table, and the showbread, which is called the sanctuary; and behind the second veil, the part of the tabernacle which is called the Holiest of All, which had the golden censer and the ark of the covenant overlaid on all sides with gold, in which were the golden pot that had the manna, Aaron's rod that budded, and the tablets of the covenant; and above it were the cherubim of glory overshadowing the mercy seat. Of these things we cannot now speak in detail.

Now when these things had been thus prepared, the priests always went into the first part of the tabernacle, performing the services. But into the second part the high priest went alone once a year, not without blood, which he offered for himself and for the people's sins committed in ignorance; the Holy Spirit indicating this, that the way into the Holiest of All was not yet made manifest while the first tabernacle was still standing. It was symbolic for the present time in which both gifts and sacrifices are offered which cannot make him who performed the service perfect in regard to the conscience—concerned only with foods and drinks, various washings, and fleshly

ordinances imposed until the time of reformation. (vv. 1–10)

The reference here is to the ceremonies that were performed
in and around the tabernacle and, later, the temple. The people are
reminded of the elaborate ceremonies and rituals that were carried
out for the atonement of sin. The author specifically mentioned
the Holy of Holies in the tabernacle and the temple, the most
sacred part of the sanctuary, where the high priest could go only
once per year, and then only after elaborate ceremonial rites of
cleansing and purification.

However, all this ritual was but a shadow, a symbol, of the ultimate atonement that would be made by Christ once for all. This is
the point the author made again and again here. He was zealous to
show that the sacrifice Christ made is perfect. We typically use the
word *perfect* to mean "without any blemish," and certainly Jesus'
sacrifice was perfect in that sense because He was the Lamb without blemish. But in biblical terms, *perfect* means "fully completed,"
and so the sacrifice that Christ made not only has no blemish associated with it; it is also perfect in terms of its completeness. It is
so complete that to repeat it would be to deny it, and that is why
all of the ceremonies in the Old Testament were discontinued in
the early Christian church. Those early believers recognized that
the former things were shadows that pointed beyond themselves,
and when the full truth emerged, to go back to the shadows was to
go back to the elemental, incomplete, and imperfect things. To go
back was a tacit rejection of the finished work of Christ. Therefore,

Christians do not celebrate an annual Day of Atonement, as did our forefathers in the Old Testament.

THE CLEANSING BLOOD

Continuing, the author of Hebrews wrote:

> But Christ came as High Priest of the good things to come, with the greater and more perfect tabernacle not made with hands, that is, not of this creation. Not with the blood of goats and calves, but with His own blood He entered the Most Holy Place once for all, having obtained eternal redemption. For if the blood of bulls and goats and the ashes of a heifer, sprinkling the unclean, sanctifies for the purifying of the flesh, how much more shall the blood of Christ, who through the eternal Spirit offered Himself without spot to God, cleanse your conscience from dead works to serve the living God? And for this reason He is the Mediator of the new covenant, by means of death, for the redemption of the transgressions under the first covenant, that those who are called may receive the promise of the eternal inheritance. (vv. 11–15)

The words "how much more" are the key to the comparison the author was making. He was not saying that A did one thing and B does another. He was saying that what B does is far more significant than what A did. B is much greater than what went before it and anticipated it.

The contrast is especially concerned with the temporal versus the eternal.

The Day of Atonement in the Old Testament was an annual thing. It was bound to the earthly calendar. The atonement that was made by Christ has eternal significance. Likewise, the Old Testament atonement took place in the earthly tabernacle. In the New Testament, the atonement is offered by the One who is the divine tabernacle, Immanuel, who pitches His tent among us. And the offering that Christ makes by His blood is not in the temple in Jerusalem, but it is in the heavenly temple, in the heavenly ultimate Holy of Holies, of which the Holy of Holies in the tabernacle and the temple were only earthly signs. Most importantly, the sacrifice that Christ made did not involve figuratively putting His blood on the mercy seat of the throne of God; it is an offering to God in His immediate presence in heaven, and it has eternal value and significance.

Next we read:

> For where there is a testament, there must also of necessity be the death of the testator. For a testament is in force after men are dead, since it has no power at all while the testator lives. Therefore not even the first covenant was dedicated without blood. For when Moses had spoken every precept

> to all the people according to the law, he took
> the blood of calves and goats, with water, scarlet
> wool, and hyssop, and sprinkled both the book
> itself and all the people, saying, "This is the blood
> of the covenant which God has commanded
> you." Then likewise he sprinkled with blood both
> the tabernacle and all the vessels of the ministry.
> And according to the law almost all things are
> purified with blood, and without shedding of
> blood there is no remission. (vv. 16–22)

Remission of sin requires a blood sacrifice. To understand that, we have to understand the significance of the blood of the sacrifice, in terms of both the animal sacrifices of the old covenant and the sacrifice of Christ in the new covenant. When God made His covenant with Noah, He gave Noah and his family the freedom to use animals for food. But He told them, "You shall not eat flesh with its life, that is, its blood" (Gen. 9:4). Therefore, the Hebrews believed that life was in the blood, so that the giving of blood meant the giving of life, while the shedding of blood meant death.

My friend John Guest once preached a sermon on the cross and the blood of Christ. He noted that Christians talk a lot about the "blood of Jesus," almost as if Jesus' blood has magical powers. We ask unbelievers, "Are you covered by the blood?" We sing, "There's power in the blood." We speak these phrases without giving much thought to what we're saying or what these phrases meant originally. That led John to say:

"Suppose Jesus had gone into Jerusalem and scratched His finger on a nail so that He bled. Would that have been sufficient to atone for the sins of His people?" He wasn't trying to be sacrilegious; he was making an important point. He went on to say: "If He scratched His finger on a nail, He might have bled, but that wouldn't have been enough to atone for our sins. Christ had to give His life as the supreme sacrifice to satisfy the demands of God's justice. When we talk about Jesus pouring out His blood, we are talking about His giving of His life. He shed His blood to such a degree that He poured out His life completely. That was the blood of the new covenant."

THE SUPERIOR MEDIATOR

Skipping ahead to the beginning of Hebrews 10, we read: "For the law, having a shadow of the good things to come, and not the very image of the things, can never with these same sacrifices, which they offer continually year by year, make those who approach perfect. For then would they not have ceased to be offered? For the worshipers, once purified, would have had no more consciousness of sins. But in those sacrifices there is a reminder of sins every year. For it is not possible that the blood of bulls and goats could take away sins" (vv. 1–4).

This is a powerful statement, one that is extremely important for understanding the significance of what happened in the old covenant and how it was fulfilled in the new covenant. The people who lived under that covenant went through elaborate rituals of blood offerings and sacrifices, and God promised to wipe away their sin as they did so. But did anything really happen? Were their sins really forgiven? The answer is an emphatic yes—they really were forgiven. But on what basis were they forgiven? Was it on the basis of the blood of animals? Absolutely not. The only thing that removed the sins from Moses and the people of God in the Old Testament was the blood of Christ. They were justified by faith in the promise looking forward. The promise was communicated through the shadows, rituals, and ceremonies that pointed beyond the blood of bulls and goats to the blood of the One whose sacrifice indeed would satisfy the demands of God's justice. By contrast, we are justified by faith in the promise that has been fulfilled once and for all in Christ, but the ground for justification is the same in both covenants.

So, at the heart of the superiority of the new covenant is the superiority of our Great High Priest, who offers the perfect sacrifice that takes away our sins forever. Earlier in Hebrews, the author took pains to show the superiority of Christ to a number of others. He is greater than angels: "For to which of the angels did He ever say: 'You are My Son, today I have begotten You'?" (1:5). He is greater than Moses: "For this One has been counted worthy of more glory than Moses" (3:3a). He is greater than the old covenant priests: "As He also says in another place: 'You are a priest forever according to the order of Melchizedek'" (5:6). The list could go on. Simply put, we have a Mediator who is not an angel, not another Moses, and not a mere priest. He is the Son of God.

This is why Paul said, "For there is one God and one Mediator between God and men, the Man Christ Jesus" (1 Tim. 2:5). This is a strange statement, because we understand that Moses was a mediator, prophets were mediators, priests were mediators, angels are mediators, and kings are mediators. So, why did the Apostle tell us that there is only one Mediator? Paul was speaking here in the ultimate sense, speaking of the One who has, within Himself, both a divine nature and a human nature. There's only one such person, who alone reaches the acme of mediation between the divine and the human. The one perfect Mediator is the one perfect Redeemer, the One who completes all of the work necessary for the salvation of His people. That is what we enjoy as participants in the new covenant, receiving all of the benefits that have been wrought for us by Christ.

CHAPTER 13

STUDY GUIDE

INTRODUCTION

The letter to the Hebrews is a letter that has experienced contortion and abuse at the hands of those who sometimes deviously, sometimes ignorantly, spread wrong beliefs that are not in harmony with other portions of God's Word. It is certainly not a simple letter, though there are doctrines clearly articulated, like, for example, the supremacy of the Messiah over all the types and shadows that preceded Him, or the necessity of faith and repentance in the life of the believer. But then there is all the talk of blood and covenants and apostasy—ideas that have led to much confusion in the church, mainly through a poor use of interpretive principles. In this chapter, Dr. R. C. Sproul seeks to clearly expound the better promises upon which the new covenant is based.

SCRIPTURE READING

Hebrews 9–10

LEARNING OBJECTIVES

1. To understand why the new covenant is founded on better promises.
2. To be able to articulate the importance of the shedding of blood in the covenants of the Bible.

QUOTATION

But as it is, Christ has obtained a ministry that is as much more excellent than the old as the covenant he mediates is better, since it is enacted on better promises.

—Hebrews 8:6

OUTLINE

I. A New and Better Covenant

A. Throughout much of the letter to the Hebrews, the author compared and contrasted the risen Christ and His old covenant counterparts.

B. In Hebrews 8, the author made clear that the new covenant is better, because it is enacted on better promises. He also mentioned the "copy" and "shadow" of the old covenant rituals that pointed to the Messiah (v. 5).

C. By way of contrast, the readers are reminded of the ancient, preexilic atoning ceremonies of the Israelite nation, and how they were to be observed repeatedly (Heb. 9).

D. But when the Messiah came, He gave the ultimate sacrifice once and for all. It was perfect in that it was without blemish and fully complete in its efficacy.

E. To repeat it by continuing to offer sacrifices is to deny this efficacy. Thus, early Jewish Christians ceased observing the ceremonial laws regarding atonement. How could they return to the copies and shadows once the ultimate fulfillment of Christ Jesus' sacrifice had come? (This, by the way, is what the author of the epistle constantly admonished his readers not to do.)

F. The key to this comparison is found in Hebrews 9:11 and following. What the new sacrifice of Christ's blood accomplished was infinitely more atoning than the old covenant ceremonies. The contrast takes these two atonements and shows how one is heavenly and infinite while the other was earthly and finite.

II. The Attestation of Blood: Hebrews 9–10

    A. The remission of sins, from the beginning of the Scriptures onward, always required the shedding of blood. Why? Because in Hebrew culture, *life was in the blood.*

    B. The giving of blood was the giving of life.

    C. Even in the garden of Eden, Adam agreed to God's stipulations, which would bring death if violated.

    D. In Hebrews 9:23 and following, we see that Christ's sacrifice superseded all previous sacrifices, for better promises required a better sacrifice.

    E. At the turn of chapter 10, the author made it clear that the blood of bulls and goats could not take away sin (v. 4). So, what was accomplished during the old covenant atonement ceremonies? Were sins forgiven? Indeed, but on what grounds? Not on the grounds of the blood of the beasts of the field, but on the grounds of Jesus' holy blood.

    F. Thus, the Old Testament saints anticipated the remission of sins that only God could provide. They had faith in His divine providence, and the atoning ceremonies of old pointed to the reality of the cross of Christ. Today, we look back to the cross and the promises fulfilled therein.

    G. But how is Jesus the *only* Mediator between God and man? Because He is the one true God-man (Greek, *theanthropos)*, the only perfect divine human to have ever lived. All previous mediators, then, could never enter the heavenlies on our behalf. Thus, the Messiah had to come in the flesh and atone for the sins of His people.

STUDY QUESTIONS

1. The new covenant is better _____.
    a. Because it is enacted on better ideals
    b. Because it is enacted on better promises
    c. Because it is enacted by a more temperate God
    d. None of the above

2. According to the author of Hebrews, the old covenant rituals _____.
    a. Were just rituals, signifying nothing in particular
    b. Were dead outward forms of worship
    c. Were copies and shadows that pointed to the Messiah
    d. None of the above

3. The intended audience of the letter to the Hebrews was _____.
    a. Gentiles scattered abroad
    b. Jewish Christians in danger of returning to the sacrificial system
    c. Jews who were not yet Christians
    d. Gentiles, Greeks, and Romans who were living in Palestine

4. Why is Christ's atoning sacrifice infinite?
    a. Because He lost no blood while on earth.
    b. Because He is the infinite Son of God.

c. Because He was killed during the Passover.

d. Because His sacrifice is repeated every time Communion is administered.

5. From the very beginning of Scripture, it was taught that the remission of sins required _____.

    a. Taking religious vows

    b. The shedding of blood

    c. Baptism

    d. None of the above

6. Why did the Messiah have to come as a human?

    a. Because humanity is the essence of perfection.

    b. To pay off a debt God owed the covenant-breakers

    c. To pay off a debt God owed the Devil

    d. What else could have mediated between God and humanity except the God-man?

DISCUSSION GUIDE

1. Describe in your own words the distinction between the covenant of redemption and the covenant of grace. Is making a distinction necessary? Why or why not?

2. In what sense is the new covenant better? Use passages from the letter to the Hebrews to support your answer.

3. In what sense is the covenant of grace essentially the same despite its various headings (e.g., the Noahic, Abrahamic, Mosaic, Davidic, etc.)?

4. Who is the administrator of the new covenant? How does He go about giving its blessings to His people?

5. Read Leviticus 17:11. What kind of atonement does this verse describe (exemplary or substitutionary)? How does this relate to Jesus' death on the cross?

6. If Jesus' death was indeed substitutionary, for what was He substituting? Was it absolutely necessary? Why? Use Scripture to support both answers.

7. Recalling our discussion in chapter 2, describe the Messiah's active and passive obedience and how they relate to the life and death of Jesus.

SUGGESTED READING FOR FURTHER STUDY

Robertson, O. Palmer. *The Christ of the Covenants*, pp. 278–300

14

THE CHRIST OF
THE COVENANT

During our consideration of the new covenant in the previous two chapters, we have focused chiefly on the ministry of Jesus. However, the one dimension of the Lord's work that I did not explore in detail is His fulfillment of the role of Adam. I want to look at this important subject in this chapter, especially considering how Jesus' fulfillment of Adam's role ties in to the original covenant of works.

First Corinthians 15 is the great resurrection chapter, where Paul showed that if Christ did not rise from the grave, the Christian faith is simply a waste of time. In what amounts to something of an interlude in the midst of this argument, he made these observations: "But now Christ is risen from the dead, and has become the firstfruits of those who have fallen asleep. For since by man came death, by Man also came the resurrection of the dead" (vv. 20–21).

This is important because one of the things that I find throughout Christendom is a failure to take seriously what Christ accomplished according to His human nature. We have a tendency to think that God came down and died on the cross in His divine nature, which, of course, would be blasphemous. We have to remember that our Mediator is the God-man, and His humanity was essential in the drama of redemption. Therefore, Paul went on to say:

> For as in Adam all die, even so in Christ all shall be made alive. But each one in his own order: Christ the firstfruits, afterward those who are Christ's at His coming. Then comes the end, when He delivers the kingdom to God the Father, when He puts an end to all rule and all authority and power. For He must reign till He has put all enemies under His feet. The last enemy that will be destroyed is death. (vv. 22–26)

Here we see Christ's work as the second Adam, as the Man who provides the remedy for the failure of the first Adam. When we looked at the covenant of creation, the covenant that God made with Adam, we saw that Adam and Eve were placed in a probationary situation. If they passed their probation and proved themselves obedient, then and only then would they receive the tree of life.

But if they violated the terms of that covenant, the penalty would be death. So, when Adam, representing all people, sinned and disobeyed God, he plunged the whole human race into spiritual death because he broke the terms of the covenant of works.

In the final analysis, the Bible teaches that there is only one way of justification—by works. You may wonder why I say that because I have long been a defender of the Reformation doctrine of justification by faith alone. How can I now say that ultimately we are saved only through works? Well, if we look beneath the surface of the doctrine of justification by faith alone, we find that it is really shorthand for "justification by Christ alone." The object of our faith is Christ, and we are justified by faith because that faith is the instrument by which we lay hold of Christ, who satisfies the covenant of works for us. Therefore, we are saved by Christ's works. We must be saved by works, but our own works simply won't do. So, we must be saved by the works of someone else. If you're trusting in your own works, you are going to perish eternally, because the only works that have ever met the standard of the covenant of creation are the works of Christ.

That's why it's so important that we believe the New Testament teaching that Jesus is the new or the last Adam, and that He did more than die for our sins on the cross. It's not simply the death of Christ that redeems us, but also His life. He did not just come to earth on Good Friday, die on the cross, and then rise from the grave a couple of days later. On the contrary, He was born as a human being, lived under and completely obeyed the law of God, and overcame temptation by Satan. During his probation, the first

Adam also was tempted by Satan, but succumbed to that temptation. Not so the second Adam. He was exposed to the assaults of Satan in very trying circumstances (humanly speaking) in the Judean wilderness. Yet Jesus was triumphant. He lived His entire life without sin.

So, at the heart of our concept of redemption is the sinlessness of Christ. That's a strange thing to me, because when people struggle with the Christian faith, the articles of our faith on which they tend to focus their skepticism are such issues as the virgin birth, the resurrection of Jesus, or the miracles of Jesus. Yet, what is more extraordinary than a sinless human life? We have no other example of that anywhere in history.

THE SINLESSNESS OF CHRIST

The sinlessness of Christ is vitally important for two reasons. First, to qualify as the One who would make the sacrifice, in order to be the sacrificial Lamb of God, He had to be a lamb without blemish. If He had sinned once, He would not have been able to atone for His own sin, let alone for anyone else's.

Second, His sinlessness is important because it describes the perfection of His obedience, obedience that is applied to us. At the heart of the Protestant controversy in the sixteenth century, and a source of ongoing controversy today, is the concept of imputation. Our salvation is based upon imputation in two ways. On the one hand, our sins were imputed—or transferred, in God's sight—to Christ when He died His atoning death on the cross.

He did not die for His sin. He died for our sin, which had been imputed to Him. But not only is our sin imputed to Christ, but the gospel, the good news, is that His righteousness is imputed to us by faith. Martin Luther correctly noted that our justification is a foreign or alien righteousness, a righteousness that, properly speaking, is not our own. It's not a righteousness that is inherent in our own persons; rather, it is someone else's righteousness. It is the righteousness achieved by the last Adam. Just as the sin of the first Adam was visited on his descendants, so the righteousness of Christ is transferred to His people.

But Christ died not only so that we could be justified. Paul told us that He "was delivered up because of our offenses, and was raised because of our justification" (Rom. 4:25). Thus, our standing before God is rooted and grounded both in the cross and in the resurrection of Christ. Jesus' resurrection was not only for Himself, but He is the firstfruits of what will be a much more extensive resurrection at His coming. We will participate in resurrection because, by raising us from death, God will vindicate the perfection of the sacrifice that Jesus made on our behalf.

One of the things that is so strange and topsy-turvy about the perspective and the worldview of the New Testament compared to the worldview of the profane and secular culture in which we live today is that modern people sneer at the Christian doctrine of the resurrection, arguing that it's impossible. They say it is scientifically untenable that a person who is really dead could come back to life. Yes, they allow for resuscitation after five minutes or ten minutes, but they have no use for our story that a Man who was in a tomb for portions of three days was brought back to life.

But while our culture judges the resurrection of Christ to be an impossibility, the New Testament asserts that it was impossible for death to hold Him (Acts 2:24). It was impossible for Christ *not* to be raised from the dead. Throughout Scripture, the problem of death is linked to sin. The reason why we all participate in death is because we all participate in sin. But if someone comes who breaks that mold, who lives a sinless life, then death has no claim on Him. Death cannot hold Him. That was the case with Jesus, so the Father demonstrated and manifested the perfection of His Son and the value of His atonement by raising Him from the dead.

That victory over death shows the victory of the new Adam over the old Adam. And as I said at the very beginning of this book, it is not simply that Jesus restores us to the position we enjoyed in the garden of Eden prior to the fall. We transcend that situation, because we participate in a victorious Adam who passed the probation and earned entrance into the heavenly place, who eats of the tree of life and gives its fruit to His people.

CONTINUITY AND DISCONTINUITY

In 1 Corinthians, Paul also discussed the age-old question of what we are going to be like in heaven. I always wonder whether I'm going to be old and overweight or whether I'll be young and fit. Will I have my same old-fashioned glasses, or will I have 20/20 vision? I hope I won't have any glasses in heaven. Paul wrote: "But someone will say, 'How are the dead raised up? And with what body do they come?' Foolish one, what you sow is not made alive unless it dies. And what you sow, you do not sow that body that shall be, but mere grain—perhaps wheat or some other grain. But God gives it a body as He pleases, and to each seed its own body" (1 Cor. 15:35–38).

Paul was saying that there is an analogy in nature. If you want grass to grow, you plant grass seed. In order for the seed to germinate, you have to kill it. You have to cover it with dirt and water it, all to the end of making the hard kernel decay and rot so that it can germinate within and bring forth life. The life that it produces in the lawn looks quite different from the seed. Paul was saying that in an analogous way, there will be continuity between this body and that which comes later. However, there will also be a radical difference, just as there is a difference between the seed and the grass.

Paul went on to say, "All flesh is not the same flesh, but there is one kind of flesh of men, another flesh of animals, another of fish, and another of birds" (v. 39). If we look around us, we see myriad kinds of living beings. Furthermore, speaking analogously, he said:

> There are also celestial bodies and terrestrial bodies; but the glory of the celestial is one, and the glory of the terrestrial is another. There is one glory of the sun, another glory of the moon, and another glory of the stars; for one star differs from another star in glory.

> So also is the resurrection of the dead. The
> body is sown in corruption, it is raised in incor-
> ruption. It is sown in dishonor, it is raised in
> glory. It is sown in weakness, it is raised in power.
> It is sown a natural body, it is raised a spiritual
> body. There is a natural body, and there is a spiri-
> tual body. (vv. 40–44)

At that point, he came back to the concept of the first and second Adams: "And so it is written, 'The first man Adam became a living being.' The last Adam became a life-giving spirit" (v. 45). Isn't that interesting? God made Adam alive, but Adam did not have the capacity to give eternal life to his progeny. But Jesus gives abundant life.

Recently I preached on John 11, the account of Jesus raising Lazarus from the grave. When Lazarus died, and Jesus got to the home of Martha and Mary too late, Martha said, "Lord, if You had been here, my brother would not have died" (v. 21). Jesus told her, "Your brother will rise again" (v. 23). Perhaps not daring to hope for an immediate resurrection, she said, "I know that he will rise again in the resurrection at the last day" (v. 24). Jesus did not contradict that statement, but He said, "I am the resurrection and the life" (v. 25a). Then He called Lazarus from his tomb.

That's the difference between the first Adam and the second Adam. The first Adam brought death. He was a living person, but all he could bring to his progeny was the corruption of death. The second Adam not only rose from the dead, but He has the power of life within Himself. He gives life to His people, which makes Him much greater than the first Adam.

Near the end of 1 Corinthians 15, Paul wrote:

> However, the spiritual is not first, but the natural, and afterward the spiritual. The first man was of the earth, made of dust; the second Man is the Lord from heaven. As was the man of dust, so also are those who are made of dust; and as is the heavenly Man, so also are those who are heavenly. And as we have borne the image of the man of dust, we shall also bear the image of the heavenly Man. (vv. 46–49)

We have borne the image of the man of dust; we go through our whole lives in this world, carrying in ourselves the corruption of Adam. We are the image of Adam as his descendants. But those of us who are born-again also bear the image of the heavenly Man, the new Adam.

SIN AND RIGHTEOUSNESS

In Romans 5, Paul reiterated this principle:

> Therefore, just as through one man sin entered the world, and death through sin, and thus death spread to all men, because all sinned—(For

until the law sin was in the world, but sin is not imputed when there is no law. Nevertheless death reigned from Adam to Moses, even over those who had not sinned according to the likeness of the transgression of Adam, who is a type of Him who was to come. But the free gift is not like the offense. For if by the one man's offense many died, much more the grace of God and the gift by the grace of the one Man, Jesus Christ, abounded to many. And the gift is not like that which came through the one who sinned. For the judgment which came from one offense resulted in condemnation, but the free gift which came from many offenses resulted in justification. For if by the one man's offense death reigned through the one, much more those who receive abundance of grace and of the gift of righteousness will reign in life through the One, Jesus Christ.)

Therefore, as through one man's offense judgment came to all men, resulting in condemnation, even so through one Man's righteous act the free gift came to all men, resulting in justification of life. (vv. 12–18)

Here we see again the concept of the shadow and the fulfillment, the typology of Adam. And again we see that just as by one man's disobedience many were made sinners, so by one Man's obedience many will be made righteous. Just as we participate in the Adamic nature in our sin and corruption, so we participate in Christ and therefore are made righteous.

It is important to remember that we are counted righteous in our justification, but in our sanctification we are actually made righteous, and the end of our salvation is our glorification. Right now we are acceptable to God because He has imputed to us the righteousness of Christ, but when He did so, He began the process of molding and shaping us into conformity to the image of Christ. He will fulfill that process in heaven in our glorification. We will get past the total failure of the first Adam because of the total victory of the second Adam.

We have seen that the very first covenant God made with humanity was the covenant of works in the garden, and Adam failed to keep that covenant. However, God did not destroy the human race completely, but He preserved Adam and his seed, and then later Noah and his family. He continued to enter into covenant relationships with Abraham, with Moses, and with David, as we have seen. But all of these covenants can be subsumed under the concept of the covenant of grace, and the covenant of grace is simply the fulfillment of the covenant of works by the new Adam. So, the covenant of works is fulfilled for us. The fact that it is fulfilled by someone else makes it gracious. We have the gift of righteousness, the gift of life, the gift of salvation because of the gift of Christ to us.

CHAPTER 14

STUDY GUIDE

INTRODUCTION

Paul made much ado about Jesus being the "second Adam." Jesus lived and died on our behalf in order to secure the blessings of the covenant once and for all. Further, if He was not resurrected then we, as the Apostle rightly noted, are the most miserable of people (1 Cor. 15:19). Jesus' going before us in all of the promises actually acts as the guarantee of those promises. In other words, because He was resurrected, we too shall see God in our flesh (Job 19:26). In this chapter, Dr. R. C. Sproul explains how Christ Jesus fully completed the covenant on our behalf, and encourages us to

anticipate with hope that final day in which we
will be raised to eternal life.

SCRIPTURE READINGS

Romans 5:12–21; 1 Corinthians 15; Hebrews 1

LEARNING OBJECTIVE

To understand the role of second Adam that Jesus fulfilled
and how His work on our behalf opens up the blessings
of heaven.

QUOTATIONS

*And beginning with Moses and all the Prophets, he
interpreted to them in all the Scriptures the things
concerning himself.... But in fact Christ has been
raised from the dead, the firstfruits of those who
have fallen asleep. For as by a man came death, by
a man has come also the resurrection of the dead.
For as in Adam all die, so also in Christ shall all be
made alive.*

—Luke 24:27; 1 Corinthians 15:20–22

OUTLINE

I. The Second Adam: 1 Corinthians 15

A. In the midst of his argument for the resurrection of Christ and the general resurrection of the dead, Paul wrote in verse 20: "But in fact Christ has been raised from the dead, the firstfruits of those who have fallen asleep."

B. Here we see that Christ is called the "firstfruits." By one man came death, so by one Man comes the resurrection of the dead; in the first Adam all have died, so in the second Adam all shall be made alive (vv. 21–23). Jesus' work is seen in light of His being the second Adam. He fulfilled or completed what the first Adam failed to do.

II. Justification by Works Alone?

A. The answer, which might be startling, is yes. Jesus was born under the law. He was tempted in the wilderness, where His probationary period is most clear. Unlike the first Adam, Jesus triumphed.

B. He was sinless, fulfilling and abiding by every aspect of the law. He kept God's covenant to the utmost. We can see from this that His sinlessness qualified Him to be a perfect sacrifice, and that He lived an absolutely perfect life.

C. This perfection is "imputed" to those whom God elected before the foundation of the world. It is "double" in nature:

1. Our sins are imputed to Christ on the cross.

2. His perfect righteousness is imputed to us. It is an "alien righteousness" (so said Luther), someone else's perfection that has come to us from the outside.

D. We are, therefore, justified by works alone—Christ's works alone. He not only died for us, but He was raised for us, as well. He was the firstfruits.

III. The Resurrection: 1 Corinthians 15

A. Because of Christ's sinlessness, it was impossible that the grave could keep Him. He served as the exemplar of our resurrection. He was the first one, and He precedes all those who will be resurrected in faith on that final day.

B. From his discussion of the resurrection of the dead, Paul moved on to a discussion about the resurrection body in 15:35ff. He pointed out that there is an analogy in nature that helps us understand this paradox: a seed's outer husk must die and decay for the life within it to germinate.

C. Just as every living thing has a body in its own kind, so the natural body differs from the spiritual.

D. In His conversation with Martha in Bethany, Jesus said that He is "the resurrection and the life" (John 11:25). Not only is Jesus alive, having been raised from the dead, but He actually has the power of life within Him. This is so because the second Adam is heavenly, while the first Adam was from the dust and returned to the dust.

E. Thus all those who are in union with Christ Jesus bear His image and are of heaven, even while our natural bodies bear the image of the first Adam and will return to the ground from whence they came.

F. In Romans 5:12ff., Paul described how through the work and victory of Jesus, we are justified once and for all, in good standing even now, awaiting our final glorification.

G. While the covenant with Adam failed because of Adam's willful disobedience, the covenant of grace succeeded and fulfilled the creation covenant through the work of the second Adam. The ultimate in grace is that this work was done in our stead. "In this is love, not that we have loved God but that he loved us and sent his Son to be the propitiation for our sins" (1 John 4:10).

STUDY QUESTIONS

1. In what sense is Jesus called the "firstfruits" in 1 Corinthians 15?

    a. He was the first to die.

    b. He was the first among all of His people to be resurrected in the flesh unto eternal life.

    c. He was the first among all people to be resurrected.

    d. None of the above

2. What does it mean to call Jesus the "second Adam"?

    a. He was the second man in history to be tempted by Satan.

b. He was a descendant of the Adamic line.

c. He was the second Jew to have ever died on a cross.

d. He fulfilled or completed what the first Adam failed to do.

3. By whose merit are Christians justified?

    a. Their own

    b. Jesus' merit conjoined with their repentance

    c. Christ's alone

    d. None of the above

4. What part of the old covenant did Jesus keep in His work on earth?

    a. He kept none of it since He established an entirely new covenant.

    b. Every jot and tittle

    c. He kept only the "moral" aspects of the covenant.

    d. Both a and c

5. How is Christ's imputation "double"?

    a. Christ's perfection is imputed to every person on earth, and only those who believe have their sins imputed to Christ.

    b. The Christian's sins are imputed to Christ on the cross, and Christ's sins are imputed to the Christian.

    c. The Christian's sins are imputed to Christ on the cross, and Christ's perfect obedience is imputed to the Christian.

    d. None of the above

6. What paradox did Paul pull from nature to describe the final resurrection of believers when Jesus returns?

    a. A seed's outer husk must never die for the life within it to germinate.

    b. A seed's outer husk must almost die for the life within it to germinate.

    c. A seed's outer husk must die and decay for the life within it to germinate.

    d. None of the above

DISCUSSION GUIDE

1. In what three mediating offices did Jesus accomplish the Christian's redemption? Pinpoint passages that describe Him in each of these roles.

2. Was Jesus mediator as God, or as man (or both)? Why is this important?

3. Who appointed Him to this office, and by whose authority did He act? Support your answer with Scripture.

4. What is meant when it is said that Jesus' being born in the flesh was an act of humiliation? What is meant when Paul wrote that He was born under the law (Gal. 4:4–5), and in what sense did He fulfill or complete it?

5. Search the Scriptures for all the various passages that attest to the fact of Jesus' resurrection, including those portions that predict the event. Why is the validity of this event so important to Paul in 1 Corinthians 15, and why is it important for us today?

6. Whose sins did the blood of Jesus atone for? Support your answer with Scripture.

7. How certain is it that God will be faithful to His promises? What proof (or guarantee) has He given that shows His utter faithfulness? Finally, and in your own words, describe some of the stories of the Bible in terms of the overarching covenantal theme found therein.

SUGGESTED READING FOR FURTHER STUDY

Vos, Geerhardus. *Biblical Theology: Old and New Testaments,* pp. 330–42

ABOUT THE AUTHOR

Dr. R. C. Sproul is the founder and chairman of Ligonier Ministries, an international Christian education ministry based near Orlando, Florida. He also serves as copastor of Saint Andrew's, a Reformed congregation in Sanford, Florida, and as chancellor of Reformation Bible College. His teaching can be heard on the daily radio program *Renewing Your Mind*.

During his distinguished academic career, Dr. Sproul helped train leaders for the ministry as a professor at several theological seminaries.

He is the executive editor of *Tabletalk* magazine and the author of more than one hundred books, including *The Holiness of God*, *Chosen by God*, *The Work of Christ*, *God's Love*, and *Pleasing God*. He also served as general editor of *The Reformation Study Bible* and has written several children's books, including *The Prince's Poison Cup*.

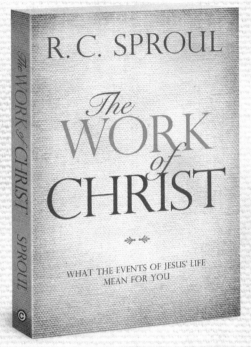 

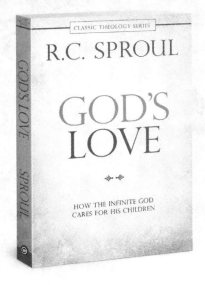
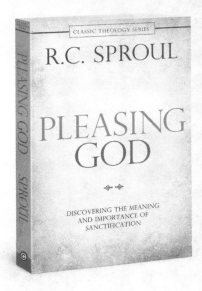